D0204658

WITHDRAWN

NIGERIA

WHAT EVERYONE NEEDS TO KNOW®

NIGERIA

WHAT EVERYONE NEEDS TO KNOW®

JOHN CAMPBELL
AND MATTHEW T. PAGE

OXFORD
UNIVERSITY PRESS

OXFORD
UNIVERSITY PRESS

Oxford University Press is a department of the University of Oxford. It furthers the University's objective of excellence in research, scholarship, and education by publishing worldwide. Oxford is a registered trade mark of Oxford University Press in the UK and certain other countries.

"What Everyone Needs to Know" is a registered trademark of Oxford University Press.

Published in the United States of America by Oxford University Press 198 Madison Avenue, New York, NY 10016, United States of America.

© Oxford University Press 2018

All rights reserved. No part of this publication may be reproduced, stored in a retrieval system, or transmitted, in any form or by any means, without the prior permission in writing of Oxford University Press, or as expressly permitted by law, by license, or under terms agreed with the appropriate reproduction rights organization. Inquiries concerning reproduction outside the scope of the above should be sent to the Rights Department, Oxford University Press, at the address above.

You must not circulate this work in any other form and you must impose this same condition on any acquirer.

Library of Congress Cataloging-in-Publication Data
Names: Campbell, John, 1944– author. | Page, Matthew T., author.
Title: Nigeria : what everyone needs to know? / John Campbell and Matthew T. Page.
Description: New York : Oxford University Press, 2018. |
Series: What everyone needs to know |
Includes bibliographical references and index.
Identifiers: LCCN 2017044619 (print) | LCCN 2017045900 (ebook) |
ISBN 9780190657994 (Updf) | ISBN 9780190658007 (Epub) |
ISBN 9780190657987 (pbk. : alk. paper) |
ISBN 9780190657970 (hardcover : alk. paper)
Subjects: LCSH: Nigeria—History. | Nigeria—Politics and government—1960– |
Nigeria—Economic conditions—1960– | Nigeria—Foreign relations.
Classification: LCC DT515.22 (ebook) | LCC DT515.22 .C35 2018 (print) |
DDC 966.905—dc23
LC record available at https://lccn.loc.gov/2017044619

1 3 5 7 9 8 6 4 2

Paperback printed by LSC Communications, United States of America
Hardback printed by Bridgeport National Bindery, Inc., United States of America

CONTENTS

2 The Economics of Oil   **46**

3 Religion   **69**

4 Politics: Nigeria's Great Game   **84**

ACKNOWLEDGMENTS

The authors would like to thank our friends and colleagues who took time out of their busy schedules to give us feedback on various sections of this book, especially Prof. Joe Abah, Sen. Datti Baba-Ahmed, Beegeagle, Joseph Croft, Judd Devermont, Michael Ehioze-Ediae, Prof. Joseph Olayinka Fashagba, Alexandra Gillies, Prof. Brandon Kendhammer, Prof. Carl LeVan, Prof. Peter Lewis, Hilary Matfess, Egghead Odewale, Oluseun Onigbinde, Prof. Ebere Onwudiwe, Ayisha Osori, Prof. Olly Owen, Aaron Sayne, Max Siollun, Katie Soulé, Prof. Alex Thurston, Jonah Victor, and Andrew Walker.

We are also grateful to everyone whose support and friendship over the years have fueled our appreciation of and interest in Nigeria, including—but not limited to—Maj. Gen. (ret.) Shehu Abdulkadir, Ahmad Abubakar, Yinka Adegoke, Ben Agande, Abiodun Ajijola, Lagun Akinloye, Emmanuel Akinwotu, Eva Anderson, Amaka Anku, Judy Asuni, Karen Attiah, Michael Baca, Gov. Attahiru Bafarawa, M.S. Darkindo, Lauren Blanchard, Patience Bentu, Christabel Bentu, Stanley Bentu, Vaughn Bishop, Amb. Johnnie Carson, Sarah Chayes, Amb. Herman Cohen, Helima Croft, Elizabeth Donnelly, Maggie Dwyer, Leanne Erdberg, Benoit Fauçon, Solomon Fehintola, Prof. Ibrahim Gambari, Idayat Hassan, Amb. Jeffrey Hawkins, Prof. Jean Herskovits, Adam Higazi, Ludovica Iaccino, Bashir Ibrahim, Jibrin Ibrahim, Amb. Godknows Igali,

Uche Igwe, Prof. Attahiru Jega, Abubakar Kari, Christina Katsouris, Sarah Kent, Prof. Darren Kew, Deirdre Lapin, Prof. Peter Lewis, Prof. Paul Lubeck, Amb. Princeton Lyman, Prof. Scott MacEachern, Daniel Magnowski, Mohammed Bello Mairiga, Sen. Salisu Matori, Angela Carson Miller, Brian Neubert, Chris Newsom, the Nigerian Studies Association, Prof. Ebe Obadare, Ernest Ogbozor, Jude Ohanele, Rolf Olson, Dapo and Ladi Olorunyomi, Prof. John Paden, Nick Parker, Joe Read, Jim Sanders, Col. (ret.) Sue Ann Sandusky, Amb. Stephen Schwartz, Prof. Laura Seay, Mausi Segun, John Sheehan, Valerie Smith, Richard Synge, Clare Thomas, Mohammed Bello Tukur, Clementine Wallop, Lesley Warner, and Y. Z. Yau.

Thanks to our current and former colleagues at the Council on Foreign Relations, especially President Richard Haass, James Lindsay, Patricia Dorff, Allen Grane, Sarah Collman, Jack McCaslin, Nathan Birhanu, Tyler Lycan, Rishav Shah, and Rachael Sullivan. Thanks also to the outstanding team at Oxford University Press, especially Angela Chnapko and Anne Dellinger.

Many thanks also to Matthew's supportive parents Barbara and David, wife Maureen, and children Teddy, Jack, and Anna.

Finally, we would like to remember our recently departed colleagues, especially Prof. Stephen Ellis, Prof. Abdul Raufu Mustapha, Ken Saro-Wiwa Jr., and Paul Stevenson.

The responsibility for the interpretations and judgments in this book is entirely our own.

ACRONYMS

APC	All Progressives Congress
AU	African Union
CAN	Christian Association of Nigeria
CJTF	Civilian Joint Task Force
CSO	civil society organization
ECOWAS	Economic Community of West African States
EFCC	Economic and Financial Crimes Commission
GDP	gross domestic product
IGR	internally generated revenue
IMN	Islamic Movement of Nigeria
INEC	Independent National Electoral Commission
IOC	international oil company
LGA	local government area
NA	Nigerian Army
NGO	nongovernmental organization
NNPC	Nigerian National Petroleum Corporation
NPF	Nigeria Police Force
NSCIA	Nigerian Supreme Council for Islamic Affairs
OPEC	Organization of the Petroleum Exporting Countries
PDP	People's Democratic Party
REC	resident electoral commissioner
SSS	State Security Service
UN	United Nations

NIGERIA

WHAT EVERYONE NEEDS TO KNOW®

INTRODUCTION

Nigeria has by far the largest population of all African countries, with an estimated one out of every five sub-Saharan Africans being a Nigerian. It is now one of the largest democracies in the world. Nigerians claim that its economy alternates with South Africa's as the continent's largest, depending on world commodity prices.[1] Nigeria has traditionally played the most active diplomatic role on the world stage of any African country. Its cultural achievements also translate into "soft" influence on other African countries and elsewhere in the world.

In 1999 Nigeria returned to civilian governance after sixteen years of military rule. Since then its trajectory toward democracy has been broadly positive in a region often characterized by civil war and arbitrary rule. Olusegun Obasanjo's presidency (1999–2007) ostensibly was civilian, though he had been a military chief of state and his style was that of a military ruler. However, his ambition to serve an unconstitutional third term was thwarted in the National Assembly, reflecting a developing elite consensus against presidents for life. Although the elections of 2007 were characterized by blatant rigging in favor of Obasanjo's hand-picked choice, Umaru Yar'Adua, the latter's presidency (2007–2010) was genuinely civilian in style and outlook. In a positive development for the rule of law, Yar'Adua, as a matter of principle, enforced judicial decisions that his administration did not like, unlike Obasanjo, who had ignored inconvenient court rulings. When Yar'Adua died in office, his vice president, Goodluck Jonathan, became president without military intervention and according to the rule of law.

If elections are taken as milestones toward democracy, as they are by most friends of Nigeria, those of 2003, 2007, and 2011 were problematic. Muhammadu Buhari—the presidential candidate who probably won the most votes in each of the three elections—was defeated by his opponent's rigging efforts. Buhari contested the outcome in the courts, which in every case unconvincingly found for the incumbent, or in the case of Yar'Adua, for Obasanjo's candidate. Nevertheless, Buhari and most of his supporters did not take to the streets, though his opponents claim his actions contributed to a deadly outbreak of post-election violence in 2011.

The 2015 election was technically better, but by no means flawless. This time Buhari's victory was beyond dispute, with the result reflecting growing concerns about the general breakdown in security associated with the jihadist terrorist movement Boko Haram and popular disgust at the rampant corruption of the Jonathan administration. Moreover, in yet another sign of a maturing democratic culture, Jonathan publicly conceded rather than contest the results. For the first time in the country's history, the civilian opposition came to power through the ballot box, arguably advancing Nigerian democracy.[2]

However, if Nigeria is a democracy, it is also a kleptocracy, a nation characterized by a type of corruption in which government or public officials seek personal gain at the expense of those being governed. Throughout the post-independence period, wholesale looting of the state by members of the political class has accelerated. On a smaller scale, corruption has become deeply embedded in virtually all aspects of national life. Chiefs of state regularly denounce this malfeasance, and President Buhari has taken concrete steps against it, but with little effect. Kleptocracy and government dishonesty have corrosive effects on popular confidence in governance. Official and unofficial corruption undermines the democratic trajectory and risks overwhelming it. It is among the most important hindrances to the country's economic and social development.[3]

With respect to its international role, Nigeria's trajectory is at present ambiguous. At the time of independence in 1960, Nigerian leaders shared the vision of a huge, democratic, diverse nation that could give Africa and Africans a place at the international high table. Indeed, for most of the country's post-independence history, Nigeria has been Africa's diplomatic leader. It has consistently participated in United Nations (UN) and other peacekeeping missions, starting with the Congo in 1960 and continuing through the current peacekeeping operation in Sudan's Darfur (which began in 2007), where it supplies the largest number of troops. It was a founder of the Organization of African Unity (OAU) and the Economic Community of West African States (ECOWAS) and later of the African Union (AU). Nigeria was an African leader in the struggle against South Africa's apartheid regime. It played an influential role in international organizations, especially the UN. In addition, individual Nigerians have provided leadership in significant multilateral settings. For example, the current secretary general of the Organization of the Petroleum Exporting Countries (OPEC) is a Nigerian, which has frequently been the case.

In the past decade, however, there has been a Nigerian withdrawal from continental leadership, mostly the result of its internal insurgencies, including Boko Haram in the northeast and militant groups in the oil-producing Niger Delta, as well as ethnic and religious conflict in the middle of the country. The logistical and other shortcomings of Nigerian participation in the international effort against a jihadist insurgency in northern Mali in 2012 perhaps marked the nadir of Abuja's regional influence. However, the Buhari government's leadership of a 2016 African multilateral effort to ease out The Gambia's authoritarian ruler, who sought to block the results of credible elections, perhaps signals the re-emergence of a Nigerian leadership role.

The post-independence economic story is even more mixed. At the time of independence in 1960, Nigeria was a major food exporter and had a flourishing manufacturing sector. The country's level of development was commonly said to be similar to that of Taiwan, Thailand, or Malaysia. As of 2017, Nigeria imports food, the manufacturing sector is largely moribund, and the transportation infrastructure is deteriorating, though efforts are underway to restore the railway network. Agricultural investment has been neglected. Despite ubiquitous cell phone use and other signs of modernity, the country is one of the poorest in the world. By indices ranging from levels of female literacy to average life span, Nigeria scores among the lowest in the world. The country's population has grown explosively without the economic and infrastructure development necessary to support it.

The negative trajectory of the post-independence economy owes much to distortions caused by sudden oil wealth without the institutions to channel it productively. Laggard institutional development reflected the militarization of governance following the 1966–1970 civil war and a series of military coups. During the long period of military rule (1966–1999, with a short interregnum), civilian institutions from the civil service to the educational system declined. Corrupt elites, with a large military component, were notably rapacious.

Nigeria's cultural achievements during the same period, however, have been outstanding. It dominates African literature, music, cinema, and drama. Nollywood, the domestic film industry, serves a continent-wide audience. So, too, does Nigerian music. Plays by Nigerian playwrights are regularly performed on Broadway in New York and in the West End in London. Nigerians now live all over the world, where they are prominent in the arts and sciences of the countries in which they have settled. Virtually every major university in the English-speaking world is host to Nigerian academics. Nigerian medical personnel are to be found in hospitals all over the United States and elsewhere, and Nigeria exports Christian clergy to the United Kingdom and the United States. Nigerians living outside of Nigeria have been notably successful in business and finance, and they are known for their entrepreneurial spirit.

Though it possesses extraordinary potential, Nigeria is truly the troubled giant of Africa.[4]

Why this book?

Nigeria is at the junction between Christianity and Islam and, more broadly, where the modern and the traditional overlap. A checkered postcolonial political history includes Africa's deadliest civil war (1966–1970) and a generation of military rule (1966–1999, with a brief, civilian interregnum). The country faces two insurrections, neither of which the Abuja government can stamp out. Yet all the while, its people retain democratic aspirations, and for the first time, the opposition won the presidency in credible elections in 2015. Its lively politics are organized nationally and within its thirty-six states (see Figure I.1). Its only rival for political and economic leadership of Africa is South Africa. But Pretoria lacks the sheer heft of Abuja, which by mid-century is likely to be the capital of one of the largest countries in the world by population. Nigeria's contemporary cultural achievements are outsized. Accordingly, this book is intended to introduce this African country that in the past was of great importance to the rest of the world and is likely to continue to be so in the future.

Though in many ways Nigeria is a proverbial "riddle wrapped in a mystery inside an enigma," its immediate importance has six elements.

- First, Nigeria is huge. It has a population that is larger than that of the Russian Federation and is already about the same as Pakistan's.[5] There are credible estimates that Nigeria's population will approach 440 million by mid-century, making it the third most populous country in the world after China and India.[6] (In 2017, the United States, with 320 million, held the third position.) Furthermore,

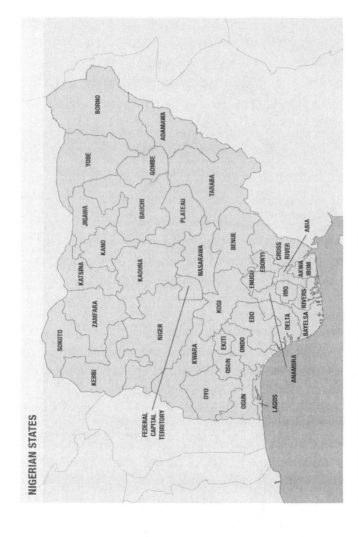

Figure I.1 Nigeria's thirty-six states. (Credit: Council on Foreign Relations)

Nigerians now live all over the world. One estimate is that 376,000 Nigerian immigrants and their children live in the United States.[7] Because of its size, Nigeria has long been a bellwether for the growth of democracy and the rule of law in postcolonial Africa.

- Second, it functions as a social and political laboratory, providing examples and lessons for other multiethnic, religiously pluralistic societies. Nigeria is an experiment in state-building and domestic peacemaking among a variety of ethnic groups and between Christianity and Islam. Nigerians commonly believe that Christianity and Islam each command the allegiance of about half of the country's population, and both are in the midst of a religious revival. Myriad traditional faiths survive, however, below the surface of Christianity and Islam.

- Third, Nigeria plays a major role in the international energy market. It is usually Africa's largest producer of oil and natural gas and is an active member of OPEC. As recently as a decade ago, Nigeria exported a million barrels of oil a day to the United States, about half of its total production. While little of Nigeria's oil now goes to the United States, it has found new markets, notably in South and East Asia, and the size of its production continues to be a major factor in international oil prices.

- Fourth, it has long been the continent's political leader. Nigeria is one of the founders of the AU and has been the linchpin of the ECOWAS. Its government contributes large numbers of troops to UN, AU, and other peacekeeping operations, and it lobbies vigorously for a permanent seat on the UN Security Council.

- Fifth, Nigeria makes major contributions to the arts, especially literature, music, and filmmaking. Its artists have an African as well as international audience. Nigeria has led the way in developing a postcolonial, African cultural identity that is distinct from that of the continent's former colonial masters.

- Finally, Nigeria's internal security challenges spill over into the West African region. The government is currently fighting the radical Islamist movement Boko Haram in the northeast, where the struggle has spread into Niger, Chad, and Cameroon. Abuja faces recurring insurrections over the control of oil revenue in the Niger Delta to the south, which influences the supply and price of oil for its neighbors. In the middle of the country (the "Middle Belt"), increasing violence over land use is exacerbated by ethnic and religious rivalries, which threaten to ignite similar conflicts in other parts of Nigeria and West Africa.

What is a Nigerian?

According to conventional wisdom, if you were to ask Nigerians who they are, you would likely get a layered answer. First, they would identify themselves with a particular family, either nuclear or extended. Next, they would volunteer religion, expecting you to do the same. Then they would note their ethnic group. They might tell you of what state they were "indigenes"—that is, where their families came from, not necessarily where they lived. And only then would Nigerians conclude that they were also Nigerian.

By and large, Nigerians identify with the state far less than Americans do. Weak identification with the Nigerian state translates into minimal loyalty to it, especially in the face of rival claims from family, religion, and ethnicity. It is the extended family, not any government institution, that provides a safety net for most Nigerians and enables their survival in times of public or private catastrophe.

Nevertheless, after almost sixty years of independence, a Nigerian sense of national identity is emerging, notably in the Lagos-Ibadan corridor in Yorubaland, the most economically developed part of the country. In other parts of the country, those who have benefited from a Western-style education and those closely associated with the federal government also identify more strongly as Nigerians. Nigerian national identity, however, remains underdeveloped in the north, the Middle Belt, and the southeast, where there has been a resurgence of support for an independent state called Biafra.

Nigerian intellectuals, including academics and journalists, have often promoted a pan-African identity rather than that of their nation-specific state, which after all was created by the colonial British. The aspiration for an overarching African unity, sometimes inspired by the Black Power movement in the United States, has underpinned the promotion of pan-African organizations such as the OAU and the AU by successive Nigerian governments as well as intellectuals.

The three largest ethnolinguistic groups in Nigeria are the Hausa/Fulani (two distinct but closely interconnected ethnic groups), the Yoruba, and the Igbo, concentrated respectively in the north, southwest, and southeast of the country. Each group has a distinctive language, material culture, assumptions about governance, legal tradition, and traditional religion. Each has its own hierarchical structure. As in traditional societies around the world, the younger people are usually subordinate to the older, and women are subordinate to men, but that can take varying forms; among the Igbo, for example, age can trump gender. An Igbo woman who lives long enough is often eligible to join the male village elders in making decisions. Furthermore, Nigerian women regularly hold cabinet-level offices in which most of their subordinates are men.

These three groups together make up only about half of the population. There are more than three hundred other ethnic groups, each usually with its own language and distinctive culture. A perennial challenge of Nigerian governance since the colonial period has been balancing among the three largest ethnic groups but also the three together against the myriad smaller groups. With more than 350 local languages, English is the only official one. It belongs to no ethnic group and therefore, in theory, to all Nigerians. It is the first language of elites, however, especially those with a Western-style education and those living in urban areas such as the Lagos-Ibadan corridor.[8]

Since independence in 1960, notions of "indigeneity" have strengthened. The concept refers to where a Nigerian has her or his traditional roots. Under certain state and local laws, indigenes are afforded special legal rights and privileges not enjoyed by nonindigenes, who nevertheless may have lived in a particular locality for generations. Hence, all Nigerians are not created equal before the law. Unscrupulous politicians sometimes exploit differences between indigenes and nonindigenes to advance a personal agenda, especially where the distinction also coincides with ethnic, land-use, and religious differences.

Nigerians like to say that their country is the world's most religious and the happiest. Those of Hausa-Fulani ethnicity are usually Muslim, ethnic Igbos are overwhelmingly Christian, and the Yoruba appear to be evenly divided between the two religions.[9]

Though Nigeria is officially a secular state, religion infuses all aspects of life, public as well as private. In 1900 it was estimated that about a quarter of the population of the geographic region that encompasses today's Nigeria was Muslim, and only 2 percent was Christian. According to an assertion by assassinated president Murtala Muhammed, these two world religions now each enroll about half of the country's population. Figures are imprecise, but there is little question that Christianity has grown explosively. Animist African religion and its magical and cultic elements, though no longer at the forefront of faith, still retain significant influence just below the surface.

What challenges does Nigeria face?

Despite its boundless human and economic potential, Nigeria faces formidable socioeconomic, security, and governance challenges. They are inescapable, according to renowned author Chinua Achebe: "Whenever two Nigerians meet, their conversation will sooner or later slide into a litany of our national deficiencies. The trouble with Nigeria has become the subject of our small talk in much the same way as the weather is for the English."[10]

A flawed democracy bedeviled by multiple insurgencies, Nigeria has nevertheless survived boom-bust economic cycles, three decades of military rule, and a catastrophic civil war. Bloated, untrustworthy, and tangled up in red tape, the Nigerian government has proven incapable of addressing the country's challenges, leaving the vast majority of Nigerians to fend for themselves.

Nigeria's socioeconomic challenges are deep-seated and multifaceted. They include rapid population growth, a lack of public services, and Nigerians' over-reliance on subsistence agriculture and petty trading to make ends meet. These problems are even more acute in underdeveloped northern Nigeria, where the socioeconomic impact of high population growth, climate change, and recent conflict has been severe.

The country is caught in a demographic catch-22: the country's rapid population growth is both a product *and* a key cause of socioeconomic stresses such as high poverty, youth unemployment, gender inequality, and food insecurity. Of the world's top ten most populated countries, Nigeria has the fastest-growing population. The UN predicts it is on track to overtake Pakistan and Brazil to become the world's fifth most populated country by 2030; by 2050 Nigeria's population will rise to almost 400 million, surpassing that of the United States.[11] Fertility rates vary widely between north and south: agrarian, overwhelmingly Muslim Zamfara State has the highest (8.1 births per woman), whereas the predominantly Christian, oil-rich Rivers State has the lowest (3.8 births per woman).[12]

Undermining Nigeria's ability to meet the needs of its growing population is the country's shortage of basic infrastructure and social services, particularly electrical power, primary health care, quality schools, clean water, and sanitation. Despite spending $14 billion on its power sector since 1999,

Nigeria (population 200 million) now generates about as much electricity as the city of Edinburgh (population 500,000).[13]

Further, Nigeria's 2016 health indicators ranked among the lowest in the world. It ranks near the bottom in infant mortality, slightly better than lawless Somalia but worse than war-torn South Sudan.[14] Just as Nigeria's public health system has fallen victim to corruption and mismanagement, so too have the country's once-proud schools and universities. Across Nigeria, private medical clinics and fee-funded private schools have proliferated, filling the void left by neglected state-run institutions. The rapid growth of Nigeria's cities and towns has overstretched their rudimentary water and sanitation systems.

Left without public services, middle-class Nigerians rely on expensive workarounds such as purified drinking water, home generators, and private school fees. Yet few working-class Nigerians—those engaged in subsistence or low-yield farming, or petty trading—can afford these necessities-turned-luxuries. Until availability of public goods increases to meet demand or its agricultural and commercial potential is unleashed, Nigeria's socioeconomic situation will worsen as demographic pressures grow.

Poor governance underpins Nigeria's economic and security challenges. Fraud, waste, and mismanagement by successive governments have exacerbated these problems, turning the surmountable into the intractable. Sluggish and haphazard government decision-making has heightened the impact of exogenous influences such as global crude oil prices and fluctuating foreign investment on Nigeria's economy.

In their quest for private gain at the expense of the public good, corrupt Nigerian officials—kleptocrats—have stoked ethnic tensions, mobilized thugs to rig elections, and used public funds as political currency. In doing so, they have warped the social contract between the Nigerian government and its citizens to the point where it now hinges on patronage rather than performance. Decades of trickle-down economic policies have created an expectation among many Nigerians that their kinsmen in government will steer public sector jobs, infrastructure projects, and cash back home. This in turn heightens the pressure on each new generation of officials to abuse their positions.

The negative effects of this breakdown in the social contract are most evident in rural and suburban areas, where government presence is weak and its positive influence on Nigerians' daily lives is minimal. The country's 774 local government councils, ostensibly responsible for delivering basic education, health, and social services, are moribund yet still gobble up more than one-third of total public spending. State governors routinely waylay these funds and set up their cronies as local government chairmen. Few Nigerians trust their local officials or think they perform well, according to a 2014 poll.[15]

In the security realm, political and governance failures have heavily impeded efforts to pacify the oil-rich Niger Delta, defend against Boko Haram terrorists in the Lake Chad Basin, and de-escalate conflicts between farmers and herdsmen. Despite living amid the source of Nigeria's great oil wealth, the people of the Niger Delta remain deeply impoverished, struggling to cope with pollution caused by gas flaring and oil spills, as well as the effects of climate change. Decades of weak and corrupt governance have fueled criminality and prevented socioeconomic development. For years, militant and criminal activity has been incentivized by elites, through either direct sponsorship or conciliatory payoffs.

In the northeastern state of Borno, government malfeasance and missteps have similarly helped transform a fringe movement into a major security threat. Ahead of the 2003 polls, state politicians recruited armed thugs to rig elections and intimidate political opponents.[16] Many of these radicalized youths later gravitated toward Mohammed Yusuf, the founder of the sect widely known as Boko Haram.[17] State leaders also wooed Yusuf, bringing some of his followers into government. When they inevitably became estranged, security forces launched a crackdown in July 2009 in which eight hundred people died and Yusuf was summarily executed. Boko Haram's surviving members went into hiding, reinventing the group as a murderous insurgency. As one security official said: "After the politicians created the monster they lost control of it."[18]

Across many parts of Nigeria, government inaction and petty corruption are sparking land disputes, particularly between farmers and semi-nomadic livestock herdsmen. While these tensions are centuries old, government efforts to co-opt and weaken traditional leadership institutions have left them less capable of resolving disagreements before they escalate into deadly violence. Self-serving state government officials fuel disputes by issuing land permits on agricultural or grazing lands in exchange for kickbacks. Unscrupulous policemen often stoke tensions by taking sides, demanding bribes, or abetting cattle rustling.

Nigeria's top security, governance, and socioeconomic challenges are not just "national deficiencies," as Achebe described, but rather complex, overlapping, and deep-seated impediments keeping Africa's most populous country and largest economy from realizing its immense potential.

What is Nigeria's promise?

Having listed Nigeria's most daunting challenges, let us turn to its inestimable promise. Far from being the dystopia portrayed in Western and, too often, its own domestic media, Nigeria at moments feels like a country on the verge of turning the corner on the path to greatness. An incredibly diverse people, Nigerians nevertheless share a common resilience, industriousness, and even optimism in the face of economic hardship, poor governance, crime, and communal conflict. Across Nigeria, the panoply of innovative local responses to disputes, economic hardship, and government dysfunction is itself an indicator of the country's latent promise.

Although the country contains an excess of ethnic and religious antipathy, Nigerians' capacity for peaceful coexistence and informal conflict resolution is too often underrecognized. Ethnic identities are beginning to soften and a stronger sense of national identity is beginning to develop among some Nigerians, according to recent Afrobarometer polling.[19]

Nigerians' capacity for intercommunal tolerance and cooperation is most easily discerned at the local level and through the lens of those who go out of their way to encourage dialogue and de-escalate tensions. In the northeastern state of Gombe, for example, security officials have in recent years gone to great lengths to convene regular meetings between farmers and herdsmen at odds over land use. Officials in neighboring states are not as proactive as in Gombe, making similar disputes there more difficult to resolve.

As the most populous country in the Africa, and one that is roughly evenly split between Muslims and Christians, Nigeria could one day serve as a global case study in peaceful religious cohabitation. Indeed, one of its major ethnic groups, the Yoruba, already does. Among Yoruba, it is not uncommon for there to be Christian and Muslim members of the same family. Even in communities deeply divided along religious lines, a few courageous Nigerians are working to promote religious tolerance and avert conflict. Imam Ashafa and Pastor James Wuye, a dynamic duo known simply as "The Imam and The Pastor," are two well-known and notable members of this cadre of community peacebuilders.[20]

Nigerians' unwavering commitment to democracy—in spite of its many flaws—is also laudable. Even though the credibility of national and state elections has varied widely, and local elections nationwide remain a farce, over 70 percent of Nigerians said in a recent poll that they would disapprove of a return to military rule.[21] Unlike in more practiced democracies, where voting takes a few minutes or can be done by mail, for most Nigerian voters casting a ballot is an all-day affair. Those voters who live and work in another part of Nigeria must return to their hometowns—which could be hundreds of miles away—to vote. On election day itself, voters typically must wait or queue for hours while election officials accredit voters singly and permit them to vote. Finally, many voters choose to stay at their polling places for several more hours to ensure their ballots are counted.

Looking beyond election day, Nigeria's democracy shows even greater promise. Both its traditional press and new media outlets are as free, dogged, and prolific as anywhere in the world. Even on the rare occasions when the government or military misguidedly tries to muzzle them, journalists are defiant and energized by the inevitable public outcry. Although nationwide demonstrations occur very rarely, the government's 2012 decision to suddenly suspend a popular fuel subsidy sparked three days of peaceful "Occupy Nigeria" protests that briefly united Nigerians across regional, religious, and socioeconomic lines; forced officials to rethink their plans; and helped expose corruption involving the subsidy.[22] Not merely displays of public anger, these protests reflected the growing capacity of Nigeria's many civil society groups. Active both nationally and across Nigeria's thirty-six states, the growing number of reputable nongovernmental organizations (NGOs) is yet another harbinger of the country's promise.

Known for its oil riches, Nigeria's economic potential remains mostly untapped. Over the last two decades, mobile phone and Internet penetration has increased exponentially, facilitating commerce and unlocking additional value across the service and agricultural sectors. Nigeria's massive and rapidly growing market for consumer goods has captured the attention of international manufacturers and homegrown entrepreneurs. More and more foreign companies are tailoring their products to Nigerian consumer preferences; one changed the formulation of its laundry detergent in Nigeria to make it lather faster and with less water after learning that local consumers think sudsy detergents are more effective.[23] Likewise, a major international brewery recently created a beer specifically for Onitsha, southeastern Nigeria's commercial capital, putting a rising sun—a cultural symbol of Onitsha's Igbo people—on the label.

Even as international companies adapt to gain a larger foothold in Nigerian markets, domestic entrepreneurs are fast becoming a major economic force. Lagos has earned the reputation for being fertile ground for innovation, especially in the creative, information technology, and commercial sectors. Many of these modern, forward-looking businesses have networked into innovation clusters, collaborating and sharing ideas and business strategies. In 2016 Facebook founder Mark Zuckerberg visited one of these clusters to learn more about Nigerian tech start-ups and look for ways to strengthen their ties to Silicon Valley.[24]

Last but not least, there are reasons to be optimistic about Nigerian foreign policy and its growing global influence. Although Nigeria has played a leading role in regional and continental affairs since its independence, its reputation suffered under corrupt dictator Sani Abacha (head of state, 1993–1998). Since Nigeria's 1999 return to civilian rule, its international profile has waxed and waned depending on presidential personality but has overall remained strong. Nigeria has served three terms on the UN Security Council over the last three decades, more than any other African country. Its sizable and relatively capable military enabled it to take an active role in UN and African-led peacekeeping missions until the Boko Haram conflict took priority, and it may yet do so again. Under Nigeria's leadership, ECOWAS—West Africa's preeminent regional organization—could become an engine for cross-border trade and economic development as well as enhanced regional security cooperation.

Throughout this book we emphasize the optimism we have about Nigeria's future by highlighting ways in which the country can unlock its great potential, whether by focusing on infrastructure development, combating corruption, reforming its military, and opening up more opportunities for women to participate in politics, or in a host of other ways.

1

HISTORICAL BACKGROUND

The history of what is now Nigeria stretches far back into antiquity. However, before British organization of the colony of Nigeria, completed only in 1914, there was no overarching cultural or political unity among what were highly disparate territories. Instead, there was a wide range of social, economic, and political differences among the populations whom the British subsequently incorporated into colonial Nigeria. The actual period of British rule was short, ending in 1960. The British legacy included the vision of a democratic polity conducted according to the rule of law, albeit one without a generally accepted understanding of what that might mean in an indigenous context. More specifically, the British left behind government institutions organized in accordance with Western, not African, experiences and values. These institutions, lacking indigenous roots—and thus popular legitimacy—did not contain or limit the post-independence ethnic, regional, and other violent competition for power and resources among elites.[1]

In 1966 two military coups temporarily destroyed the civilian administration and resulted in the death of prominent political leaders from the late colonial political elite. The resulting civil war in 1967–1970 between the federal government and the army of the breakaway nation of Biafra is the great national tragedy of Nigeria's postcolonial history.[2] Between 500,000 and 2,000,000 people—many of them children—died from the resulting disease and starvation. Thereafter, with the exception of a short civilian interregnum (known as the Second Republic in 1979–1983) under Shehu Shagari, the military ruled Nigeria continuously from 1966 until 1999. In that latter year the military leadership and a broad coalition of political elites orchestrated the election of a nominally civilian government under retired general (and former military chief of state) Olusegun Obasanjo.[3] Since then, civilian government has endured and has gradually become more democratic in style and tone. Following credible elections in 2015, in which opposition leader Muhammadu Buhari came to power, many observers argue that Nigeria is now a democracy in practice as well as in name.

Before it was a European colony, what did Nigeria look like?

The British created Nigeria out of various territories with little more in common than that they shared the same colonial master and geographic proximity. The languages, cultures, and institutions of government in each of these territories were different. So, too, was their art, among the most sophisticated ever produced.

Among the earliest distinct civilizations in what is now Nigeria was that of the Nok people, centered in what is now the Middle Belt and the northwest of modern Nigeria. Economic life included iron smelting as well as agriculture. Established as early as 900 BCE, their civilization survived until about 200 CE, when it mysteriously disappeared. They were characterized by a highly advanced judicial system with a hierarchy of courts. However, they are best known now for their magnificent, often life-sized, terracotta sculptures. Some anthropologists argue that they influenced the development of later civilizations. Their artistic achievements are a source of contemporary pan-African pride.

Yoruba civilization is also perhaps two thousand years old, though its relationship to Nok civilization is unclear.

Traditional religion remains especially strong and undergirds Yoruba Islam and Christianity. In what is now the southwest of Nigeria, the Yoruba organized city states; they were the most urbanized people in sub-Saharan Africa before the later nineteenth century. These Yoruba city states periodically consolidated into an empire, of which Oyo (ca. 1400–1895) is usually considered the most politically powerful. (See figure 1.1.)

Another Yoruba political entity was Ife, ruled by a kinglike figure ("Ooni"). Ife remains a repository of Yoruba culture, religion, and art. Millions of descendants of Yoruba slaves live in Brazil's northeast, and an estimated forty million Yoruba live in Nigeria and adjacent states. They continue to recognize the Ooni in some sense as their spiritual leader. Internecine warfare among the Yoruba city states provided the opening for the British occupation of Lagos in 1861.[4] A state characterized by ethnic diversity was the walled city of Benin. A monarch ("Oba") with powers similar to those of the Ooni ruled over the Kingdom of Benin, home of a magnificent artistic tradition, bronze casting.

The Igbo kingdom of Nri in the far south was administered by a priest-king with religious rather than political power. It eschewed state violence and was a haven for escaped slaves. There were also small collections of quasi-autonomous towns and villages in the southern Niger Delta and elsewhere that were increasingly transformed and victimized by the emergence of the transatlantic and trans-Saharan slave trade.

In the Hausa-speaking north, a succession of empires emerged that were increasingly Islamic in character and oriented toward the trans-Saharan gold, copper, and slave trades. The most prominent of these before the British occupation in 1902 was the Sokoto Caliphate, established in 1806 (see figure 1.1). It was not only a sophisticated Islamic state with cadres of officials and scholars by the time of its defeat by the British in 1902, but had also become the largest remaining slave empire in the world.[5] Geographically, its domain included northwest Nigeria as well as adjacent territories in what is now Niger. The sultan presided over a feudal court, with

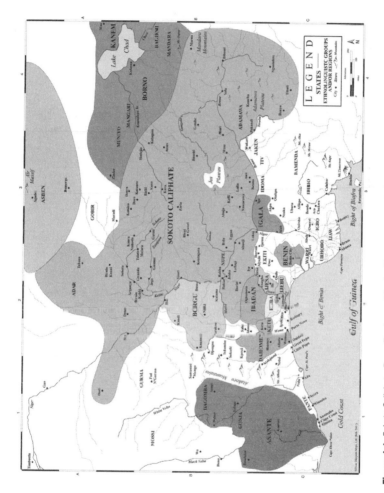

Figure 1.1 Sokoto Caliphate, Borno Empire, and Yoruba States ca. 1840. (Credit: Henry Lovejoy)

subordinate emirs. The legal and judicial system was based on Islamic law, sharia. The sultan was usually recognized as the most senior Islamic figure in Nigeria and occupied the first position in terms of official protocol among traditional leaders nationwide.

The second largest—and much older—precolonial Islamic state was the Bornu Empire, ruled over by the shehu of Bornu. Centered in northeast Nigeria, its largest city is now Maiduguri (see figure 1.1). The domain was structured in a manner not unlike Sokoto. The shehu had subordinate emirs and enforced a version of sharia law. Like the sultan of Sokoto, the shehu's dominions extended beyond the boundaries of modern Nigeria and included parts of what are now Chad, Cameroon, and Niger. When Bornu was in its expansionist phase, the sultan of Sokoto tried to conquer it but failed. The predominant language in Bornu remained Kanuri, while in Sokoto it was Hausa and, among Fulani elites, Fulfulde. In both empires, the British governed through the indigenous institutions established under the sultan and the shehu.

Islamic traditional rulers still exercise significant power over their subjects, though they are not recognized by Nigeria's secular constitution. High Islamic culture was present in the empires and emirates in the north, and large numbers of ancient manuscripts with superb calligraphy have survived from the Middle Ages. (The dry climate is conducive to their preservation, as was the Islamic principle of equal inheritance, which ensured that they were widely scattered throughout the region.) The Islamic empires in the north were oriented toward horsemanship, cattle herding, and trans-Saharan trade. Today, Islamic traditional rulers continue to conduct regular *durbars*, celebratory manifestations of their feudal pomp based on horsemanship.

In the far south, by contrast, the individual village was sometimes the primary political unit. The multiplicity of languages present in the south discouraged political unity. The region is the point of origin of the diverse Bantu family of languages. Adjacent villages' dialects are often mutually unintelligible, mitigating against the emergence of larger political units. Livelihood was largely dependent on fishing and farming, rather than on raising livestock. Political units were often small, with governance exercised by local councils of elders. In some communities women—once they achieved advanced age—could join these leadership bodies. The absence of building stone and clay suitable for brick making encouraged the emergence of a vibrant artistic tradition based on cloth, costume, and basket making.

How did the slave trade impact Nigeria's development?

There was significant contact between Europeans and the peoples of the coast long before the British organized the colony of Nigeria. The Portuguese were trading with the coastal peoples as early as the fifteenth century, notably with the Kingdom of Benin (not to be confused with the modern Republic of Benin, which is west of Nigeria). The Portuguese especially sought gold, slaves, and copper; from them, the Africans purchased salt, textiles, and weapons. The Portuguese even sponsored a Roman Catholic mission that enjoyed temporary success. The Benin kingdom was well organized and powerful; its trade relationship with Europeans was one of equals. Subsequently, Benin was strong enough to abolish the slave trade with Europeans, though its people maintained the trade among themselves. (European slave traders developed alternative slaving networks.) Benin high culture is probably best known by Europeans and Americans from its superb bronze sculptures, displayed notably at the Metropolitan Museum of Art in New York, the British Museum in London, and the Louvre in Paris.

By the late sixteenth century the transatlantic slave trade had become the most important link between Europeans and what is now West Africa and Nigeria. The slave trade involved the forced deportation of twelve to fifteen million Africans to the Western Hemisphere during the four hundred years it was active.[6] Following the abolition by Brazil of the transatlantic slave trade in 1831, thousands of former slaves returned from Brazil, resettling in Lagos from the 1830s onward. Many of these ex-slaves—known locally as *aguda*—and their descendants prospered, evolving into Lagos's mercantile middle class. Even in today's multicultural Lagos, evidence of their influence—Afro-Brazilian architecture, Portuguese surnames like Da Silva, and even an annual carnival—survives.

The trans-Saharan slave trade lasted longer than the transatlantic, though its total numbers were smaller. It is estimated that the trans-Saharan slave trade trafficked up to seven thousand slaves each year from the tenth through the nineteenth centuries, for a total of as many as nine million people. In general, trade, not just in slaves, tied northern Nigeria culturally to North Africa and the Middle East.[7] The demographic consequences of the two slave trades are subject to academic debate. Some scholars see the trades as resulting in the permanent underpopulation of the continent and a significant contributor to its slower rate of material development compared to Europe and North Africa. Others, however, see the demographic consequences as marginal. However, there is little doubt that the trade promoted violence and the destruction of traditional societies wherever it operated.

All along the Slave Coast—the littoral fringes of the Gulf of Guinea and Bight of Benin—Europeans established forts from which they bought slaves from African middlemen. However, Europeans were too weak, and indigenous governments were too strong, for the Europeans to establish colonies there as they did in North or South America. European vulnerability to African disease, notably malaria, also thwarted any potential European settlement.

European domination of the slave trade moved from the Portuguese to the Dutch to the French and the British, reflecting shifts in the balance of power in early modern Europe. By the eighteenth century the British dominated the trade from the Gulf of Guinea but continued to depend on African coastal middlemen for slaves. In the nineteenth century European public opinion came to oppose slavery, and European governments often justified their formal occupation of West Africa on the basis of the imperative to suppress the slave trade. By then, unlike in the seventeenth and eighteenth centuries, the balance of firepower firmly rested with the Europeans, as the poet Hillaire Belloc pointed out:

Whatever happens,
We have got the Gatling gun,
And they have not.[8]

Some European trade goods even became indigenized; for example, London bowler hats became a part of the traditional dress of the Ijaw people of the Niger Delta. The Muslim emirates in what is now northern Nigeria continued to be deeply engaged in the trans-Saharan slave trade into the twentieth century, three generations after the transatlantic trade had been suppressed.

Except for the coastal areas, what is now Nigeria was largely free of any European penetration before the nineteenth century. Travelers from the Middle East occasionally visited medieval northern Nigeria, and Muslims from the Sahel could and did make the pilgrimage to Mecca. Nevertheless, until the mid-nineteenth century, European maps of West Africa, including Nigeria, were largely blank, except for the slave trading posts along the coast. Accordingly, much of the story of precolonial Nigeria is the domain of anthropology, oral history, myth, and tradition.

What was Nigeria's colonial experience, and how did it win independence?

According to nineteenth-century historian John Robert Seeley, Britain acquired its empire—including its Nigerian colony—haphazardly: "in a fit of absence of mind."[9] Colonial expansion was driven by numerous preoccupations, including the anti-slavery movement, episodic rivalry with French and German territorial ambitions, and private commercial interests. It was informed by the epoch's thoroughgoing racism, justified by "science" as Charles Darwin's views on natural selection were bowdlerized into "social Darwinism."

The British acquired Lagos and the surrounding area in 1861 in the aftermath of the collapse of traditional Yoruba political structures and the resulting chaos that appeared to threaten African Christian converts and European economic interests. Some twenty years later Westminster acquired the southeast under pressure from the private Royal Niger Company and to preclude German expansion of their Kamerun (now Cameroon) colony.

The British first occupied the north between 1900 and 1903 to block possible French penetration and to end the slave trade. Westminster consolidated these disparate territories into a single entity—"Nigeria"—only in 1914 for their own administrative convenience; amalgamation simplified His Majesty's government's budgetary and tax processes. Flora Lewis—the colonial editor of the *Times of London* and later the wife of the first colonial governor, Lord Frederick Lugard—invented the name "Nigeria." (The national anthem at the time of independence in 1960 was also written by a British expatriate.)

The colonial period was comparatively short. Modern Nigeria was consolidated under King George V, the monarch in power during World War I (1914–1918). Forty-six years later, panicked by the anticolonial war in Algeria and the emergence of an independence movement in Gold Coast (Ghana) led by Kwame Nkrumah, Westminster wound up its Nigerian colony in 1960. In Nigeria there was no independence-era equivalent of Mahatma Gandhi or the Congress Party of India with a post-independence national vision that resonated across ethnic and religious divisions. Instead, what agitation there was for independence involved a small cadre of mostly Lagos-based politicians, including Herbert Macauley, Anthony Enahoro, and Obafemi Awolowo, which never grew into a mass political movement. Pro-independence sentiment was even weaker in the north.

However, the most prominent independence-era politicians, Nnamdi Azikiwe (an ethnic Igbo), Awolowo (Yoruba), Ahmadu Bello (Fulani), and Abubakar Tafawa Balewa (Fulani), did share the vision of "the Nigeria project." (See figures 1.2–1.4.) Its central idea was that a united, democratic Nigeria, conducted according to the rule of law, would be big enough to give Africa and the black diaspora a seat at the table with larger powers. At the same time, the four represented and

Figure 1.2 Nigeria's first president, Nnamdi Azikiwe, as depicted on the 500 naira note.

Figure 1.3 Northern region premier Sir Ahmadu Bello. (Credit: US Department of Energy Archives)

Figure 1.4 Western region premier Obafemi Awolowo. (Credit: Eliot Elisofon Photographic Archives, U.S. National Museum of African Art)

promoted ethnic and regional interests at the expense of a national vision.

If many Nigerians appeared unenthusiastic about independence, by the mid-twentieth century colonialism was no longer popular among the British, and successive Westminster governments feared the specter of a colonial war that could be exploited by the Soviet Union.

Thus, British rule in Nigeria lasted little more than three generations, and its social impact was superficial, especially in rural areas. In contrast, the British Empire in India lasted for 280 years (1667–1947); in Virginia it lasted 169 years (1607–1776). As mentioned previously, tropical diseases—especially malaria—largely precluded European settlement in Africa; some colonial officials were not Europeans but rather Africans from other parts of the empire. Representatives of British business interests were similarly often from other parts of the empire, notably India and Hong Kong, and included Lebanese and Greek immigrants.

Colonial administration of the "modern" economy (based on cotton, palm oil, groundnuts, and other food crop exports) and of British subjects and expatriates was based on British common law and statute. British courts functioned much as they did elsewhere in the empire. "Native" administration, however, involving most of the population, was characterized by a practice known as "indirect rule." Associated with the first royal governor of Nigeria, Lord Frederick Lugard, indirect rule was a governance strategy that involved making use of indigenous rulers, institutions, and legal systems. (British governance in Nigeria recalled the more developed system of indirect rule in parts of India.)

For example, the British retained the emirate system of government in the north and recognized Islamic sharia law in the religious, family, and criminal domains. However, they refused to allow those punishments that offended British sensibilities, such as amputation and stoning. Sharia never applied to British subjects or expatriates, and in theory, appeal from sharia courts to British courts was possible, though it was unusual and expensive. Nor did indigenous rulers exercise authority over British subjects. The result was a variety of legal systems, though with recognition of the preeminence of British common and statutory law. Nevertheless, very few Nigerians ever came into contact with a British colonial official, let alone British justice. Few Nigerians ever laid eyes on a European during the colonial period.[10]

While the British discouraged European missionaries from proselytizing in the north, they encouraged them elsewhere. With the missionaries came modern science and technology, education, and medicine. Hence, while the north remained yoked to the emirate system with its medieval aspects, as though preserved in amber, other parts of the country moved into the modern world. This reality is at the root of the disparity in economic and social development between the north and the south today.

Because of indirect rule, the British did not seek a monopoly over violence. Native authorities wielded a variety of coercive powers against their subjects. The British did, however, organize a national police force and, eventually, an army. The purpose of both was to maintain internal order, which they did through the rough methods that persist today. Only toward the end of the colonial period did the British establish a network of secondary schools and a single university, Ibadan, then closely associated with the University of Cambridge. Nor did they move to establish institutions of self-government until the last few years before independence.

Driven by almost yearly conferences in the later 1950s, London designed the move of the country toward independence with a small number of emerging Nigerian politicians. British administration, especially during its last years, was efficient—not especially corrupt—and successfully maintained law and order. The British established an apolitical indigenous civil service. The postal service also worked well, and more than fifty years after independence, Nigerian judges still wear the full-bottom wigs of the British judiciary.

In the post-independence era, Nigerian intellectuals have tended to see the colonial experience as malign. Their argument is that the colonizers put in place government institutions and practices that destroyed traditional self-rule. The British, so the argument goes, pursued economic initiatives that created harmful incentives and fed the corruption that so disfigures contemporary Nigeria. Popular hatred of the colonial state carried over to suspicion and fear of the post-independence government of Nigeria and is largely responsible for the alienation of the Nigerian people from Abuja, or so that argument runs.

However, a revalorization of colonialism appears to be underway, led by Chinua Achebe in his final book, *There Was a Country*, published shortly before his death in 2013.[11] At a concrete level, Achebe recalled the personal security and efficiency of public services, especially the postal service, under the British.

He suggested that British educational initiatives in Nigeria have been underestimated. From the political perspective, he argues that the British attempted to form an orderly, coherent political state. But their efforts were undermined by their too-rapid move toward independence. It is difficult to know how far this revisionist view of colonialism will spread. However, in contemporary Nigeria, seemingly racked by corruption, insurgency, and crime, and in which service delivery is minimal or nonexistent, it is not unusual to encounter nostalgia for colonial rule among many who would not consider themselves intellectuals.

What caused the Nigerian Civil War, and why is it still important?

The 1967–1970 civil war, often called the Biafra War, was a national tragedy. Its impact on the national psyche is comparable to that of the 1861–1865 American Civil War. Nigeria's recovery, however, was much faster, thanks to the leadership of chief of state Yakubu Gowon and his policy of national reconciliation, helped along by the postwar oil boom, which provided the funding necessary for reconstruction. Moreover, for a generation, memories of the horrors of the civil war acted as a brake on ethnic separatism and political extremism.

At independence, Nigeria's government had the form of a British-style democracy, with Queen Elizabeth II as head of state within the Commonwealth. Shortly after independence, the country transformed itself into a republic, with a Nigerian, Nnamdi Azikiwe, an ethnic Igbo, replacing the queen as head of state in 1963. (Azikiwe had also been the last governor general of Nigeria under British rule.) Despite the symbolic change, Nigeria remained an enthusiastic member of the Commonwealth. Economic and cultural ties with the United Kingdom remained close, from Westminster's perspective a short-term vindication of its strategy of rapid decolonization.

However, the essentially foreign, British political institutions were not strong enough to contain the rampant political and ethnic jostling for power and wealth. Politics was dominated by elite ethnic and regional competition with little regard for broader national interests. The three leading political figures were Obafemi Awolowo, from the west; Abubakar Tafawa Balewa, from the north; and Nnamdi Azikiwe, from the east. Awolowo was premier of the western region,[12] held numerous offices at the federal level, and ran for the presidency three times, unsuccessfully. Tafawa Balewa was the last chief minister of the British colony and the first prime minister of an independent Nigeria. Azikiwe was independent Nigeria's first chief of state, an office that was largely ceremonial. All three were leaders of the independence movement, and all three founded political parties. Though they were Nigerian nationalists to a greater or lesser extent, none was a politician who appealed successfully across ethnic and religious boundaries. Post-independence, delivery of government services deteriorated, and in the western part of the country there was widespread political violence associated with elections.

In January 1966 a group led by mid-ranking, mostly ethnic Igbo officers staged a bloody coup against the allegedly northern- and Muslim-dominated civilian government, killing, among others, Prime Minister Abubakar Tafawa Balewa and Ahmadu Bello, the premier of the region of northern Nigeria. In July 1966 a group of predominantly northern officers launched a bloody mutiny-turned-counter-coup, in which military head of state J. T. Aguiyi-Ironsi was killed. In the aftermath Yakubu Gowon—then a thirty-one-year-old lieutenant colonel—emerged as the military head of state. A Christian, Gowon was from a small tribe in the Middle Belt and had close ties to the northern, Muslim elite. He remained in office for nine years, through the civil war and reconstruction.

Against the backdrop of the 1966 coup and counter-coup, a major massacre against Igbos living in Nigeria's majority-Muslim north took place. In response, there was a mass flight of the Igbo to the southeast, their traditional homeland. The serious attempts to negotiate a meaningful, federal system to address Nigeria's diversity failed. Under the leadership of Lieutenant Colonel C. Odumegwu Ojukwu, Igbo-dominated southeastern Nigeria (Biafra) declared independence in July 1967. However, Ojukwu sought to incorporate into Biafra the oil-rich, non-Igbo Niger Delta. These areas resented Biafran domination, weakening the newborn state from the beginning.

Both sides in the civil war were led by military governments, that of now general Gowon in Lagos, and that of now Biafran general Ojukwu in Enugu.[13] Neither government was democratic, and both committed human rights abuses during the war. Biafra was explicitly Christian in its rhetoric and mounted a sophisticated propaganda campaign targeting Europe and the United States. Biafran propaganda portrayed the war as a struggle between Muslims and Christians and raised the specter of genocide should the Igbo lose. It is still widely claimed among the Igbo that the federal government used starvation as a deliberate instrument of war. The international image of the Biafra War came to be that of a starving child.

Though more secular, the Nigerian federal government was painted as Muslim dominated, even though many Christians occupied key positions in its ranks. Nevertheless, the federal war effort benefited from the then-superb Nigerian civil service, which did much to ensure the continued functioning of government. Fighting was initially heavy. Eventually federal forces were able to cut off Biafra from the outside world and squeeze it to extinction, despite a highly publicized international airlift of supplies that captured the Western imagination. Ojukwu fled the country on the eve of Biafra's military defeat by federal forces in January 1970.

The British, Soviet, and American governments nominally favored the federal side, while France, apartheid South Africa, and a few African states rallied around Biafra. However, official outside involvement was minimal. By contrast, Biafra became a popular cause in Europe and the United States, where it was often associated with the civil rights movement. It was private individuals and organizations rather than governments that conducted an airlift of supplies to Biafran forces, prolonging the war by several months.[14]

The prewar massacre and Biafran propaganda convinced many that a federal victory would result in a bloodbath against the Igbos. However, Gowon insisted on a policy of postwar national reconciliation in which there were to be "no victor, no vanquished." He made it stick. Military discipline was also notably better than outsiders had anticipated, and there were no postwar mass killings. At one level, economic recovery from the war was very rapid, as was reintegration of Biafra into Nigeria at all levels. However, ethnic Igbos still widely believe that they are excluded from the highest levels of Nigerian life, and there has been no Igbo president. In periods of economic and political difficulty, pro-Biafra sentiment resurges among many Igbo.

Many Nigerians saw Biafra as a Christian cause, and the churches and clergy in Biafra often supported independence. After the war was over the federal military government moved to nationalize and secularize the mission schools and hospitals established by various denominations. Their quality declined precipitously. Only during the civilian presidency of Olusegun Obasanjo (1999–2007) did the churches and private organizations regain the right to establish and run schools and hospitals. But the government did not return to the churches the schools and hospitals that it had seized.

The Biafra War led to the militarization of federal politics, reinforcing the preeminent role of the army in public life and facilitating a hollowing-out of civilian political institutions by successive military governments, including the civil service and the educational system. At about the same time, immense amounts of revenue from oil and natural gas came online. However, the country lacked the institutional capacity to manage its new wealth. The line between the military and "businessmen" blurred. Corruption and income inequality, already high, reached dizzying heights as colonels with access to oil contracts became rich. The table was set for a generation of military government.

What lessons can we learn from the fall of the Second Republic?

Military head of state Yakubu Gowon consistently said that his goal was the restoration of civilian, democratic government, as had existed before the coups of 1966. However, when he appeared to back away from that commitment against a backdrop of increasingly flamboyant corruption, a group of military officers ousted Gowon in a largely bloodless coup in 1975.[15] They were led by Joe Garba, Murtala Muhammed, and Olusegun Obasanjo. Murtala Muhammed—a dynamic and left-leaning officer—subsequently became head of state.

In February 1976 Murtala Muhammed was assassinated in a Lagos traffic jam (or a "go slow") during a botched coup led by Lieutenant Colonel Buka Dimka, an officer from the same small ethnic group as Gowon. The military leadership then designated a reluctant Obasanjo as the chief of state. (See figure 1.5.) He orchestrated a return to civilian governance through a new constitution, the result of broad consultation, resulting in multiparty elections, held in 1979. The international community widely praised Obasanjo for his seemingly voluntary handover of power to a civilian government.[16]

The new constitution was broadly modeled on that of the United States. It substituted a presidential system of government for the previous Westminster system and established a weak form of federalism with the creation of states.[17] In constituent assembly debates that led to the new constitution, the role of sharia polarized Muslims and Christians. While sharia in the criminal domain was not established under the Second Republic, the groundwork was laid for its later implementation on a state-by-state basis under the Fourth Republic (1999–present) in the predominantly Islamic north.

The presidential victor in 1979 was a secondary school science teacher and former finance minister from the north, Shehu Shagari, an ethnic Fulani. His principal opponents were Obafemi Awolowo, the Yoruba statesman, and Nnamdi

Figure 1.5 Olusegun Obasanjo, military head of state from 1976 to 1979 and civilian president from 1999 to 2007. (Credit: The White House)

Azikiwe, the Igbo former president. Shagari's inauguration marked the beginning of the Second Republic (1979–1983).

The new constitution provided for the American practice of direct election of a president who was both chief of state and head of government. But changes in constitutional arrangements and different personalities did not address the institutional weaknesses and lack of administrative capacity of the Nigerian state. The principal political parties continued to have an ethnic base: Awolowo's was Yoruba, Azikiwe's was Igbo, and Shagari's was Fulani. Corruption proliferated, and law and order broke down in some parts of the country. Inequality of wealth increased, as did the conspicuous consumption of champagne and other imported luxury items by corrupt officials and their cronies.[18]

Existing economic and social tensions were exacerbated during the Second Republic by a dramatic—if cyclical—fall in oil prices that reduced government revenue. In response, Shagari cut the federal budget; sought the assistance of the International Monetary Fund (IMF); and expelled some two million Ghanaians who had come to Nigeria to work and, so it was alleged, took jobs away from Nigerians.

Shagari was re-elected president in 1983 with 47.5 percent of the vote; once again his two principal rivals were Awolowo and Azikiwe, and all three ran on the tickets of ethnically based parties. The elections were widely regarded as rigged. A military coup on New Year's Eve 1983 overthrew the Second Republic and replaced it with a federal military government. General Muhammadu Buhari became military head of state, and Shagari was placed under house arrest. Eventually the deposed president was cleared of personal wrongdoing, and he was released in 1986. However, he was banned for life from participating in politics.

There are lessons from the trajectory of the Second Republic. One is the enduring influence of the democratic vision. Gowon ultimately precipitated the coup by backing away from a commitment to restore civilian, democratic government. The coup, the subsequent administration of Olusegun Obasanjo with his preparation for the return to civilian democracy, and the establishment of the Second Republic with elections in 1979 show the continued importance to the country's political class of the "Nigeria project." The elites were willing to accept authoritarian governance that promoted and protected their interests, but only if the ideal and goal of democracy provided what was essentially a fig leaf.

The 1983 overthrow of the Second Republic shows, however, that the roots of civilian democracy remained shallow and good governance elusive. Political activity continued to be largely shaped by ethnic and, increasingly, religious identities, as demonstrated by the debate over the role of sharia. That same political class viewed the Nigerian military with which it overlapped as the ultimate guarantor of the Nigerian state when things went wrong. When poor governance and corruption undermined the state against the backdrop of falling oil prices, the military in conjunction with the political class was prepared to step in, to "punish" the civilian politicians. Shagari's fall was greeted with public rejoicing in the short term. However, the military was set to rule Nigeria until 1999.

Why did the military rule Nigeria for so long, and what was its legacy?

The military governed Nigeria from 1966 until 1999, interrupted only by the short civilian Second Republic (1979–1983) and an abortive transition, the Third Republic (1992–1993). Nevertheless, the military always maintained that its tenure was temporary, and military chiefs of state were careful to insist that they were "preparing" for the restoration of civilian democracy, even if their personal commitment to it was as shallow as their pecuniary interest in the status quo was deep.

During the period of military government the chief of state was always a senior military officer, as were the governors of the states. National and state assemblies were suspended. But military chiefs of state, by no means unlimited in their authority, were responsible to the Armed Forces Ruling Council, which was sometimes divided.[19] Most of the rest of the government personnel were not in uniform. There was considerable continuity in government administration. The court system preserved a quasi-independence, and human rights and other NGOs remained active, though frequently subject to official, if informal, coercion. The Nigerian Bar Association functioned as one of the most influential human rights organizations in the country during this time.

Respect for human rights varied considerably from one military regime to another, with the nadir reached under Sani Abacha (1993–1998), who jailed his opponents on spurious grounds and sanctioned judicial and extrajudicial killing, even if only on occasion. Throughout the period of military rule critics would sometimes "disappear" or die in "automobile accidents." The military controlled the press and other media mostly through intimidation rather than overt violence or censorship. For example, if a periodical printed a piece displeasing to the authorities, they would shut it down for two or three days, thereby destroying its profitability for a month. By such methods the military achieved effective self-censorship.

Nevertheless, for Nigerians "on the street," freedom of speech endured, and while they did not live in a democracy, they were not subject to violent, military authoritarianism either. This was in part because of the lack of bureaucratic and security service capacity. In effect, the military leadership had merged with the political class. Prominent personalities moved easily between the military and big business, and military rank could be a ticket to great wealth. It was the military that controlled the oil revenue. Especially during the Babangida and Abacha years, corruption accelerated, tying the otherwise ethnically and religiously divided political class beneficiaries ever closer together.

Moreover, the military co-opted, neutralized, or eliminated potential centers of civilian opposition, if haphazardly. It bloated the civil service and the universities with its own appointees, starved both of funding, and overtly coerced critical organizations such as the Academic Staff Union. The civil service was weakened, in part by watering down entry requirements. Political parties of the Second Republic were banned and then reconstituted in different forms by military governments, in theory to replace ethnicity and regionalism with parties having a national focus. Under Babangida, the regime created two political parties—the Social Democratic Party (SDP) and National Republican Convention (NRC)— by fiat, "one a little to the left, the other a little to the right." These parties had no particular ethnic or regional identity and no real policies beyond getting their candidates elected when civilian government was restored. The delivery of the most basic government services, such as mail and healthcare, rapidly deteriorated. Much of today's poor governance and administration has roots in the generation of military rule.

Moreover, military rule did not guarantee stability. In 1985 General Ibrahim Babangida led a successful coup against General Muhammadu Buhari and became military chief of state. (Buhari subsequently became the civilian president of Nigeria in 2015.) Babangida, too, launched preparations for a return to civilian government, culminating in presidential elections in 1993. However, when wealthy Yoruba businessman Moshood Abiola, the "wrong" candidate from the military perspective, won, Babangida annulled the elections.[20] He then stepped down, perhaps voluntarily, to be replaced by General Sani Abacha, who in turn died in 1998 under suspicious circumstances.[21]

Throughout the period of military rule, coup rumors were rife. Nevertheless, with the exception of the two in 1966, military coups in Nigeria have been remarkably bloodless.[22] They were carried out by members of the same coterie of senior officers, who were colleagues and friends. In effect, they replaced one another in high office through coups rather than by rigged elections. The loser typically went abroad, to return a few years later with a pension and his accumulated wealth intact. None was ever tried for abuse of office in these senior officer coups, but there was considerable anxiety within the political class about the possibility of a junior-officer-led coup, like the one led by Jerry Rawlings in 1979 in Ghana. Such a coup could be a populist attack on privilege.[23] Indeed, a junior officer coup nearly succeeded in Lagos in 1990, prompting Babangida to move his administration abruptly to the unfinished capital of Abuja. Coup makers sometimes justified themselves as forestalling a junior officer move, evidence for which was always obscure.

The military era ended following the death of Abacha in 1998. The political class, by then heavily military in its composition and orientation, decided to reduce popular unrest by restoring the form of democratic institutions even while preserving its entrenched privileges. Without any popular referendum, it imposed a new constitution, modeled on that of the Second Republic. The country's most influential politicians organized themselves into the People's Democratic Party (PDP) to run in nationwide elections held in 1999. A party generally seen as "a little to the right," the PDP chose former military head of state Olusegun Obasanjo, a Yoruba Christian retired general from the southwest, as its candidate. Obasanjo's choice was a nod to the country's Christian population, as most of the military chiefs of state had been Muslim, as well as to the Yoruba, in recognition that M. K. O. Abiola—winner of the annulled 1993 presidential election—was an ethnic Yoruba.

Obasanjo's presidential opponent, Olu Falae, campaigned for a political grouping "a little to the left"; he too was a Yoruba Christian. The military viewed Obasanjo, one of their own, as no threat to their fundamental interests. They ensured he was rigged into office. International and, to an extent, domestic opinion was satisfied that the process had led to the formal departure of the military from office. However, the elections themselves were so corrupt that former president Jimmy Carter, an election observer, left the country to avoid appearing to endorse them.

Though the military established a civilian government and "returned to the barracks," it never renounced its self-defined vocation as the last guarantor of the state in the event of crisis. Successive civilian governments have neglected the military, in part to reduce their potential for coup making.

Among many Nigerians today, the ills of the country are ascribed to the "twin evils" of colonialism and a generation of military rule. As we have seen, a revalorization of the period of British rule is underway. The same has not happened with respect to the string of military governments; although the British have left, the Nigerian military remains waiting in the wings.

Who are Nigeria's most important historical figures?

Nigeria lacks a unifying, popular icon such as George Washington, Simón Bolívar, Charles de Gaulle, or Nelson Mandela with which to promote national identity. Although each of Nigeria's ethnic groups venerates precolonial figures— usually emirs, kings, and chiefs—as important historical figures, few such individuals are broadly admired.

Historians might put Samuel Ajayi Crowther (1809–1891) and Herbert Macauley (1864–1946) in this category. A liberated slave, Crowther was a distinguished educator and missionary who in 1864 was consecrated as the first African bishop in the Anglican Church. His grandson Macauley was an outspoken critic of British colonial rule in early twentieth-century Lagos and sought to promote a Nigerian sense of identity to unite the country's many ethnic groups. A popular yet controversial figure, Macauley established Nigeria's first political party in 1923.

Society and governance from the colonial period until the present has been organized into patronage/clientage networks, a system called "prebendalism."[24] Prominent politicians have been the leaders of such networks, which often have an ethnic, religious, and regional cast. The most important political leaders have represented the interests of specific regions and ethnic groups rather than appealing to the nation as a whole. Intentionally or not, they in effect have protected the status quo rather than promoted the change that would benefit nonelite Nigerians. Independence was no political or social revolution, nor has there been one since. Nigerians often consider the three fathers of independent Nigeria to be Obafemi Awolowo, Nnamdi Azikiwe, and Ahmadu Bello.[25] Bitter personal rivals, they nevertheless articulated the "Nigeria project" together. They tried to be nation builders, but all three were compromised by their ethnic identities.[26]

They were all well-educated: Awolowo at the Inns of Court in London; Azikiwe at Columbia and Howard Universities, among others, in the United States; and Ahmadu Bello at the Katsina Teachers Training College, probably the most rigorous academic institution in northern Nigeria. All three served as premiers of their respective regions, into which the country was divided in the later colonial and early independence periods: Awolowo of the Yoruba-dominated western region, Ahmadu Bello of the Fulani-dominated north, and Azikiwe of the Igbo-dominated east. Azikiwe became the first governor general of an independent Nigeria, a largely ceremonial position; Ahmadu Bello was the first post-independence premier, the head of government, until he was murdered in the first coup of 1966.

All three founded or dominated political parties, Awolowo the Action Group (AG), Azikiwe the National Council of Nigeria and the Cameroons (NCNC), and Ahmadu Bello the Northern People's Congress (NPC). The three parties represented sectional and regional interests with little national appeal and were primarily personal vehicles to advance the ambition of their leaders. Of the three leaders, perhaps Azikiwe and his party were the closest to advocating a nonethnic, reformist agenda; for example, his party called for free healthcare and education for all children nationwide.

None of the three was able to subordinate ethnic identity to a national vision. Awolowo was a founder of Egbe Omo Oduduwa, a mass organization devoted to the preservation and advancement of Yoruba culture. At the height of his political influence, the Yoruba political elite designated him "leader of the Yorubas." Ahmadu Bello was one of the highest-ranking traditional leaders in the emirate north. The 1966 coup makers killed him because they alleged that his goal was northern and Muslim domination of Nigeria. Azikiwe progressively asserted his Igbo identity and eventually supported an independent Biafra.

As a member of the generation that followed Awolowo, Azikiwe, and Ahmadu Bello, Chukwuemeka Odumegwu Ojukwu (1933–2011) pursued a military rather than civilian career. He was from the late colonial elite, and his father was said to be one of the richest men in Nigeria. Ojukwu was educated at Oxford. Following the 1966 coup, the military government made him the premier of the eastern region. He subsequently led the independence movement and became the Biafran chief of state. Following defeat, he went into exile in 1970. He returned to Nigeria in 1982, following a pardon from civilian president Shehu Shagari, and played an active role in shaping and promoting Igbo identity politics until his death in 2011.

After 1966 the military heads of government were J. T. Aguiyi-Ironsi (1966), Yakubu Gowon (1966–1975), Murtala Muhammed (1975–1976), Olusegun Obasanjo (1976–1979), Muhammadu Buhari (1983–1985), Ibrahim Babangida (1985–1993), Sani Abacha (1993–1998), and Abdulsalami Abubakar (1998–1999). Civilian presidents have been Shehu Shagari (1979–1983), Olusegun Obasanjo (1999–2007), Umaru Yar'Adua (2007–2010), Goodluck Jonathan (2010–2015), and Muhammadu Buhari (2015–).

Of the military chiefs of state, the most noteworthy was Yakubu Gowon, who led the national government to victory in the civil war and at its conclusion instituted a policy of "no victor, no vanquished" that promoted national reconciliation. Another military leader, Ibrahim Babangida, introduced economic reforms and started a process that was to result in the restoration of civilian rule following the 1991 elections. These elections were postponed to 1993, and the results were ultimately annulled, further delaying civilian rule. Furthermore, corruption soared to new heights on his watch. Finally, Sani Abacha was known for his brutality, human rights violations, and epic corruption.[27]

In the aftermath of the civil war, the military had a stronger sense of national Nigerian identity than other stakeholders and continued to see itself as the ultimate guarantor of the survival of the Nigerian state. Military chiefs of state downplayed ethnic and religious identities. They wore military uniforms rather than ethnic, civilian dress. They avoided being photographed entering or leaving mosques or churches. Officers' clubs served alcoholic beverages nationwide, even in states where Islamic law banned it. Of the five military chiefs of state, two were from large ethnic groups, Obasanjo (Yoruba) and Buhari (Fulani), while three were from small ones: Gowon, Babangida, and Abacha.

Since the restoration of civilian governance, presidents have come from the larger ethnic groups: Obasanjo is a Yoruba, Yar'Adua was a Fulani, Jonathan is an Ijaw, and Buhari is a Fulani. The relative ranking of the size of the largest ethnic groups is contentious among Nigerians. Conventional wisdom is that the Hausa and Fulani are the largest ethnic bloc in numbers, followed by the Yoruba, the Igbo, and then several of the most sizable "minority" groups (e.g., Tiv, Ijaw, Kanuri, Bini, and Ibibio).

2

THE ECONOMICS OF OIL

Despite its huge agricultural potential and flourishing service sector, Nigeria's economy remains addicted to petroleum revenues. They are one of the country's few sources of foreign exchange, indirectly drive many other sectors of the economy, and account for almost all government income. As global crude oil prices have fluctuated over the years, the Nigerian economy has experienced dizzying booms and gut-wrenching busts. This dynamic is unlikely to change unless federal and state governments rein in wasteful spending, invest in the country's infrastructure and human capital, and implement policies that facilitate growth. Until they do, Nigeria's economy will struggle to realize its enormous potential.

How big is the Nigerian economy, and what does it look like?

Nigeria's economy is just that: big. Since an effort in 2013 to resurvey and recalculate its gross domestic product (GDP), Nigerians can boast of having the largest economy in Africa, larger than that of South Africa, Egypt, or Kenya. Its economy is also surprisingly diversified, despite its government's continuing overdependence on petroleum revenues. Nigeria's economy undoubtedly will continue to grow over the coming decades, though perhaps not as fast as its population, which is on track to be the world's third largest by 2050, according to UN estimates.

In 2016 the World Bank estimated Nigeria's GDP was US$415 billion, making it the twenty-sixth largest in the world and just larger than those of Iran and Thailand, and a bit smaller than Poland's and Belgium's. Yet because of Nigeria's colossal population, its GDP per capita amounted to a mere $2,260 per person in 2016. Looking at the Nigerian economy through this lens, it looks nothing like Belgium's, instead ranking 132nd globally, just below Sudan and Papua New Guinea. It is important to keep in mind, however, that there are many different ways to look at the size and composition of the Nigerian economy. Moreover, our understanding is shaped by statistics, financial information, and census data that are not always reliable or complete.[1]

Other economic indicators paint a gloomier picture of the Nigerian economy. The country fell into recession in 2016, its economy contracting as global crude oil prices fell. Nigeria's stock market hit an all-time high in 2014 but has declined sharply since then. Its currency, the naira, was Africa's worst-performing currency in 2016, plummeting almost 37 percent despite government efforts to prop up its value. As a result of this drop and other factors, the country's inflation rate has steadily increased, rising to 18.5 percent at the end of 2016. For the average Nigerian, food, housing, water, fuel, and education costs increased sharply. The cost of dietary staples like rice, palm oil, and garri (cassava) doubled—or in some parts of the country tripled—over the course of 2016.[2]

Nigeria's recent economic malaise has brought its government's long-standing over-reliance on the petroleum sector into sharp focus. The oil and gas sector yields over 70 percent of government revenues but accounted for only 8 percent of GDP as of late 2016. Despite it being the country's cash cow, policy drift and government mismanagement have bedeviled the petroleum sector. Nigeria's sprawling, aging oil infrastructure has enjoyed minimal new investment in recent years, due in part to falling oil prices but also to security, corruption, and regulatory concerns.

Keen to reduce government dependence on oil revenues, President Buhari promised in his inaugural speech to reinvigorate the country's mining sector. Despite tapping one of his best ministers to lead the effort, it has yet to take off. Unlike some of its West African neighbors, such as gold-rich Ghana and Mali or Guinea—one of the world's top bauxite producers—Nigeria has yet to attract international mining operators.[3] Instead, the government hopes to develop the country's iron ore deposits to lower the cost of raw materials used to make steel. This would in turn help drive domestic industrial expansion. Plans to build new coal-fired power plants might also lead to the revival of dormant mines in the hills above Enugu, still known as the "Coal City."

Like its mining industry, Nigeria's manufacturing sector has bottomed out after a long period of decline. The sector has contracted steadily since its heyday in the late 1980s and now accounts for less than 10 percent of GDP. Several factors have contributed to its decline over the years, including the country's substandard transport and power infrastructure, rampant corruption and red tape, high borrowing costs, import bans and foreign exchange shortages, erratic regulatory and economic policies, and increased foreign competition, especially from Chinese manufacturers.[4] Those state-owned industries hastily established in the heady days of Nigeria's boom years, often with little thought given to their long-term viability, became "white elephants," unprofitable and likely to remain so. Compounding their drain on the economy, corrupt officials used them as tools for spreading patronage and embezzling state funds.

Nigeria's agricultural sector is its largest, accounting for roughly 30 percent of GDP. The sector employs more people than any other but is dominated by small-scale and subsistence-level farming. Nigeria's land tenure laws, which give corruption-prone state and local government officials the power to grant—and revoke—occupancy rights, discourage farmers from investing in long-term improvements to their plots. As a result of this and other obstacles, Nigeria has very few mechanized, well-irrigated, industrial-scale farms.

Government efforts to boost agricultural production—of which there have been many over the years—have had mixed results. The Anchor Borrowers' Program, recently launched by the Central Bank of Nigeria, reportedly has stimulated rice and wheat production in several states by providing affordable loans to subsistence farmers. The program helps farmers ramp up production to commercial levels and connects them to companies that can help them process and market their crops.[5] On the flip side, a major government drive during the last decade to promote the cultivation and domestic consumption of cassava—a starchy tuber—was a notorious failure. Between 1980 and 2010 corrupt officials reportedly embezzled billions of dollars budgeted to buy fertilizer for struggling farmers.[6] And in spite of government efforts to reduce fertilizer fraud, official corruption remains a major obstacle to the modernization of Nigeria's agricultural sector.

Beyond the emergence of a modern agricultural sector, the growth of Nigeria's services sector will be key to Nigeria's long-term economic growth, given that the service sector accounts for roughly 50 percent of GDP. The country's telecommunications, financial services, information technology, and entertainment industries have all boomed over the last decade, becoming pillars of the country's non-oil economy. This success comes despite the fact that Nigeria is a difficult operating environment: it ranks 169th out of 190 countries on the World Bank's ease of doing business index, below economic basket case Zimbabwe and only marginally better than war-torn Syria.[7] In addition to traditional economic mainstays like long-distance trading and market and street-based retail activities, Nigerian e-commerce is set to expand as smartphones become cheaper, allowing Internet retailers like Jumia, Konga, and Payporte to expand their market penetration.

How does Nigeria's oil and gas industry work?

Nigeria's petroleum industry is a complex contrivance that is riddled with challenges yet remains critical to its public finances. It produces about two million barrels of crude oil per day, though militant attacks, vandalism, and infrastructure failures often drive output lower. Focused onshore from the late 1950s until the early 2000s, more than half of all crude oil production has since shifted offshore as international oil companies (IOCs) chase higher profit margins. Although Nigeria has the second-largest crude oil reserves in Africa, its petroleum sector has stagnated due to rising costs, regulatory problems, and insecurity in the oil-rich Niger Delta. Nigeria's natural gas reserves rank among the ten largest worldwide, but the country has struggled to exploit them for electrical power generation or export and flares about 75 percent of gas associated with crude oil production.[8]

Nigeria's oil and gas industry consists of three sectors: upstream, midstream, and downstream. The upstream sector is the industry's main focus; it centers on the exploration and production of crude oil and natural gas. After wellheads disgorge crude oil from the ground, it is typically gathered together via a manifold and piped to a separator, which removes water and gas from oil. While the gas is either flared or sent to be processed, the crude oil typically is transported by pipeline to tank farms, domestic refineries, or floating production, storage, and offloading (FPSO) vessels anchored offshore. The upstream sector relies heavily on services provided by support contractors, such as seismic mapping, welding, drilling, construction, logistics, and security.

At this point the extracted oil and gas enters the midstream sector. Crude oil designated for export is transferred ("lifted") by tanker vessels for onward sale. Although most Nigerian crude oil is sold directly onto world markets and transported to refineries in Europe, Asia, and elsewhere, some is refined domestically. Nigeria's four state-owned refineries—rendered virtually moribund from years of mismanagement and corruption—remain unable to meet the country's rapidly growing downstream demand for consumable fuels like petrol, kerosene, jet fuel, diesel, fuel oil, lubricants, cooking gas, and petrochemicals. This gap has been filled by the black market and by small-scale, heavily polluting, artisanal refineries in the Niger Delta that illegally refine ("cook") stolen crude oil to produce rudimentary diesel fuel. Until the government privatizes its refineries or private investors build new ones, Nigeria must continue to import almost all the refined petroleum products it consumes.

Once the oil has been refined domestically—or more likely, internationally—it enters the downstream sector. Unlike the upstream sector, in which international companies continue to play a major role, domestically owned ("indigenous") firms dominate the downstream. Heavy regulation and corruption surrounding the importation, distribution, as well as the (at times costly) subsidy, of gasoline and kerosene has led to episodic shortages and a perpetuation of the black market fuel trade. Looking beyond its maze-like network of pipelines, flow stations, and export terminals, Nigeria's oil and gas industry is also made up of numerous government entities, as well as both international and indigenous oil companies.

Foremost among these is the country's state oil company, the Nigerian National Petroleum Corporation (NNPC)—a name synonymous with corruption among Nigerians. The NNPC is a powerful behemoth; it sells up to one million barrels of crude oil a day, or almost half of the country's total production. Middlemen companies given juicy contracts to "lift" crude oil on behalf of NNPC conduct most of these sales.

International oil companies typically produce crude oil as part of a joint venture in which the NNPC is the majority shareholder or as part of a production-sharing contract. In addition, the NNPC exerts influence over national petroleum policy, spends lavishly on itself with minimal oversight, and regulates most aspects of the petroleum industry: all clear conflicts of interest and out of step with international best practices.[9] It also (mis)manages the country's refineries and operates several subsidiaries, such as the upstream-oriented Nigerian Petroleum Development Company (NPDC) and the downstream-focused Pipelines and Product Marketing Company (PPMC), among others.

The Ministry of Petroleum and its Department of Petroleum Resources (DPR) is another key player. It awards the lucrative oil prospecting licenses (OPLs) and oil mining licenses (OMLs) for the country's more than three hundred oil blocks. The ministry oversees several parastatals and an alphabet soup of other agencies, including the Petroleum Products Pricing Regulatory Agency (PPPRA), which sets the official price of gasoline, kerosene, and the like, and the Petroleum Technology Development Fund (PTDF), which funds professional education and training for Nigerians seeking to work in the petroleum industry.

Able to wield unparalleled influence over all sectors of the industry, Nigeria's petroleum ministers frequently use their power to enrich themselves and their allies. This position is so important that several presidents have held onto it, dual-hatting themselves. One former minister allegedly embezzled several billion dollars using a variety of schemes, while another stands accused of awarding an oil block to a company he secretly controlled. Instead of conducting rigorous oversight to forestall such schemes, legislators and officials at other ministries often abet them in exchange for a piece of the action.

On the commercial side of the equation, five IOCs—Exxon Mobil (United States), Royal Dutch Shell (The Netherlands), Total (France), ENI (Italy), and Chevron (United States)—remain heavily invested in Nigeria, especially in deepwater exploration and production as well as onshore natural gas projects. The IOCs—in joint venture with the NNPC—continue to dominate the upstream sector despite facing high production costs; challenging regulations; and security threats like militancy, piracy, pipeline vandalism, and crude oil theft.

Even so, indigenous oil companies now enjoy a greater stake in the industry than ever before, filling a void left as IOCs have divested from onshore, swamp, and shallow water fields. The long-term viability of many of these Nigerian-owned companies remains uncertain, however. Several are struggling to stay afloat amid lower prices and production disruptions, while others face scrutiny from anticorruption investigators.

Looking ahead, is Nigeria's petroleum industry likely to work any better than it does now? Probably not. Many of its shortcomings—corruption, mismanagement, regulatory uncertainty, insufficient investment, insecurity in the Niger Delta—have yet to show sustained improvement. Although legislators in 2017 passed a version of the long-delayed Petroleum Industry Bill, it does not go far enough to reform and reduce uncertainty in the country's oil and gas sector. Until Nigerian leaders decide to bring the NNPC up to global standards and put an end to corrupt and inefficient practices that discourage investment, the sector will continue to underperform.

Have Nigerians benefited from the country's enormous oil wealth?

Some Nigerians have benefited, but too few. Beyond Lagos Island's modern skyline and Abuja's gaudy villas, most Nigerians are struggling to make ends meet as subsistence farmers or in the commercial hustle of the country's cities and towns. Poverty is especially severe in northern Nigeria, an area whose demographic and socioeconomic indicators rank among the most challenging in the world. Nigerians invariably blame officials, past and present, for squandering and embezzling decades of oil riches.

As oil became a quick and easy source of huge amounts of revenue, successive governments failed to pursue policies and projects designed to ensure sustainable development of the formal, non-oil economy. Instead, they wasted billions of dollars on short-term spending sprees, government patronage, and self-enrichment schemes. Oil revenues became a "national cake" to be shared out as soon as it was sliced.

To better understand the impact of Nigeria's oil wealth, let's first look at how this national cake is shared. Government revenues—over 70 percent come from petroleum—are divvied up each month among the three tiers of government according to set percentages: the federal government (52.68%), 36 state governments (26.72%), and 774 local governments (20.60%). These figures represent revenue allocation for the month of November in 2016.[10] Nine oil-producing states[11] receive an additional "derivation" payment totaling 13 percent of the oil revenue they generate. These states'[12] derivation payments amounted to a whopping 4.19 trillion naira (roughly $26.2 billion in 2014 dollars) over fifteen years (1999–2014).

Looked at individually, Nigeria's states have populations and budgets comparable to those of small countries. With the exception of Lagos State, however, they have minimal internally generated revenue (IGR). They instead depend on monthly allocations of government income to make ends meet. The size of each state's allocation is determined by a complex formula that takes into account its population, land mass, IGR, and other socioeconomic factors. Each state's monthly payout changes based on fluctuating government revenues, sundry deductions or additions, and any changes to the other variables.

Nigeria's top-down, feast-or-famine funding model provides few incentives to federal, state, and local government entities to perform effectively, develop their own sources of revenue, or be parsimonious with their spending. Endemic government corruption, ill-conceived policies, and lack of transparency and independent oversight have further diminished the degree to which the country's vast oil wealth has been used to benefit, never mind transform, Nigerian lives.

Unlike Indonesia or many of the Persian Gulf states, Nigeria did not use its petrodollars to build and maintain public facilities—such as transportation and power infrastructure—that its non-oil economy needed to flourish. Instead, Nigerian officials have relied on disproportionately high recurrent expenditures, mainly salaries and other perks, as a patronage tool. While this has modestly expanded the ranks of middle-class Nigerians who can afford private schools, clinics, and generators, it has immiserated the majority of Nigerians, who lack access to basic necessities.

The result of the victory of private gain over public good is readily apparent: Nigeria's stubbornly high poverty rate is perhaps the clearest indicator that the country's oil wealth has failed to trickle down. Between 1980 and 2010, the percentage of Nigerians living in poverty increased from 27 percent in 1980 to 69 percent in 2010 according to the government's own statistics.[13]

Poverty rates are higher in rural areas and across much of the country's semi-arid north, where high fertility rates, illiteracy, high unemployment, and food insecurity are both a cause and a consequence of endemic poverty. On the UN's Human Development Index, which measures life expectancy, education, and living standards, Nigeria ranks 152nd out of 188 countries.[14] Taken on its own, northern Nigeria would likely rank closer to neighboring Niger, at the bottom of the list.

While poverty remains acute across the country, the share of Nigerians considered middle class—which varies widely depending on how that term is defined—is growing. While an often-cited report used economic statistics to determine that 23 percent of Nigerians are now middle class, others point to more qualitative indicators. Novelist Elnathan John sums up what it means to be middle class:

> Forget what foreign economists say. . . . In Nigeria, a person who is able to purchase a generator for personal use and run said generator every time power goes off is a member of the middle class. . . .

Members of Nigeria's middle class however are those who never have to tell you "I could have called you but I don't have credit." . . .

Middle class Nigerians can afford movie tickets, often for themselves and their families or lovers as frequently as once every week . . . [and] can also afford the overpriced popcorn that is traditionally part of the cinema experience. . . .

A middle class Nigerian often has a car . . . [and] is often able, albeit through much complaining, to buy very expensive fuel from the black market to keep their car running. . . .

The middle class, while still cherishing the immense power of God, know the truth in the saying: God helps those who help themselves. A middle class Nigerian is one who knows a person in government or authority who can change the course of events in their favor. . . .

Middle class Nigerians, however take pride in their travels. They invest in their travels. They talk about where they have been and show off items they bought from abroad.[15]

Yet even as the ranks of popcorn-buying Nigerians grow, income inequality remains acute. Over the last few decades Nigeria has consistently scored above 40 on the Gini scale[16], ranking it in the top 25 percent of countries in which the income gap between rich and poor is greatest.[17] Across Nigeria's states, average household incomes vary widely. Sokoto State, in the country's Sahelian northwest, is Nigeria's poorest: more than 80 percent of people live in absolute poverty.[18] Even Lagos State, home of Nigeria's commercial capital, has millions of extremely poor residents despite having the highest per capita income of any state.

Capital flight—the expatriation of wealth, both legal and illegal—is another key reason Nigeria is not benefiting from its oil wealth. This financial drain has ebbed and flowed over the years, depending on the strength of the country's economy and currency, as well as global crude prices. At times, the outflows have been astronomical: $22.1 billion was transferred out of the country during a five-week period in late 2014 as foreign investors soured on Nigeria's flagging economy and wealthy Nigerians sought to protect their assets from currency devaluation.[19]

During Nigeria's oil booms, corrupt outflows peaked as kleptocrats stashed billions of dollars in offshore accounts and used stolen oil revenues to buy luxury properties abroad. A former oil minister suspected of embezzling billions of dollars faces domestic and international corruption charges, while several other ex-officials stand accused of stealing millions from state coffers. Experts conservatively estimate that these illicit financial flows out of Nigeria between 2004 and 2013 totaled $178 billion.[20]

How can Nigeria grow its economy?

Nigeria's failure to realize its economic potential is more a failure of governance than it is a result of the country's addiction to oil revenues. Due to its swelling population, even high rates of economic growth during boom years have done little to transform the lives of Nigeria's citizens, many of whom scrape a living by engaging in subsistence agriculture or small-scale commerce. In the words of the emir of Kano, himself a former central bank governor:

> Successive governments in Nigeria have since independence in 1960, pursued the goal of structural changes without much success. . . . Since then, the economy has mainly gyrated with the boom-bust cycles of the oil industry. Government expenditure outlays that are dependent on oil revenues have more or less dictated the pace of growth of the economy. Looking back, it is clear

that the economy has not actually performed to its full potential particularly in the face of its rising population.[21]

To kick-start the country's economy and stabilize its long-term growth, the Nigerian government should roll back failed policies and practices that have held it back. Equally important, officials at all levels need to work together to provide public goods and services—especially education, healthcare, transportation, and power—that the economy needs to thrive. To afford these changes, they must cut wasteful spending, reduce political patronage flows, and rein in state governments' unsustainable financial practices.

The first step toward reinvigorating Nigeria's economy would be for the government to reverse several shortsighted macroeconomic, trade, and monetary policies. Statist and protectionist, these policies were intended to insulate the economy from external pressures but have instead stifled free enterprise and foreign investment, deepening the government's dependence on oil revenues while also failing to protect middle- and working-class Nigerians from the effects of rising inflation. They have also combined to make Nigeria one of the world's least competitive economies globally; it ranks near the bottom of the World Economic Forum's Global Competitiveness Index, just above basket case Venezuela.[22]

Among its macroeconomic challenges, Nigeria's currency woes are perhaps the most critical and difficult to address in isolation. The value of the naira has spiraled steadily downward: roughly at parity with the US dollar in the mid-1980s, it recently slipped as low as 500 to the dollar. Like its predecessors, the Buhari government has reacted by tightening foreign exchange controls and quixotically spending billions of dollars to prop up the nation's beleaguered currency.

Although well intentioned, this decades-old approach has facilitated corruption, empowered black marketeers, and stifled international trade while at the same time failing to reduce Nigeria's dependence on imports, given the many other obstacles facing the country's manufacturing and agriculture sectors. To reduce pressure on the naira over the medium to long term, Nigerian officials need to cultivate non-oil sources of foreign exchange by diversifying the export economy and eliminating barriers to foreign investment, instead of fruitlessly trying to micromanage monetary policy in the face of global headwinds.

To achieve these policy shifts, the Nigerian government will need to invest more in the building blocks of a resilient, diversified economy. Even as the federal and state governments have spent billions on roads, railways, ports, electrical power, schools, hospitals, universities, and other economic enablers, they have realized few gains. By inflating contracts, soliciting kickbacks, and mismanaging budgets, corrupt officials have derailed countless such projects.

The privatization of Nigeria's power sector, for example, was deeply flawed, resulting in the balkanization of the country's unprofitable power sector among several companies—many controlled by former politicians—that lacked the resources, regulatory freedom, and supporting infrastructure (e.g., transmission lines and reliable natural gas supplies) needed to turn it around. Until officials embrace meaningful procurement reforms and more transparent budget and contracting processes, they will continue to fall short in delivering what Nigeria's economy needs to grow.

If global crude oil prices struggle to rebound, Nigeria will be unable to make these transformational investments unless its leaders drastically cut wasteful federal and state government spending, merge or eliminate dozens of costly agencies and parastatals, and move to reduce risky subnational borrowing. Doing so, however, will require a shift in Nigerian political culture away from the widely held view that government is a public employment program and a mechanism for dividing up the "national cake" (i.e., petroleum revenues) among the country's geopolitical and ethnic constituencies.

To start, the federal and state governments should cull their herds of what economists call "white elephants": state-owned enterprises like the dilapidated oil refineries and steel mills, among many other companies, that sap government budgets over long periods, even if they incur huge losses. Similarly, officials need to wind down nonessential government agencies. For example, even in the midst of economic recession Nigeria spends $13 million annually on its Atomic Energy Commission, despite not possessing a single nuclear power plant. It also budgeted $5 million for its new Defense Space Agency, whose multiple civilian counterparts—including the ambitiously named Space Transport and Propulsion Center—already gobble up $30 million annually.[23]

Even if the federal government rethinks its budgetary priorities, Nigeria's future economic trajectory hinges heavily on whether its state governments follow suit. By law, state and local governments receive almost as large a share of national revenues—most of which come from the petroleum sector—as the federal government gets. Yet roughly half of all states are unable to cover their recurrent expenses—salaries, pensions, and other operating costs—using the revenue allocation they receive.[24] Rather than cutting wasteful spending, many states take out loans to cover the difference.

States' borrowing trends are risky and need to be addressed, according to a recent report by the African Development Bank.[25] Rising national borrowing and increasingly unsustainable subnational debt are underappreciated obstacles to economic growth. Many state governments are now deep in the red, having borrowed during boom years to fund expensive but nonessential projects like local airports, monorails, and tourist resorts. Even though Nigeria's national debt is still relatively low by global standards, fiscal federalism means that if states default on their debts, the federal government is on the hook.

With its long-term growth jeopardized by misguided policies, corruption, and infrastructure shortfalls—not to mention global market pressures—Nigeria's economy needs a complex set of remedies to grow at a rate sufficient to put it on track toward future prosperity.

How does Nigeria fit into the global economy?

Other than crude oil, enterprising emigrés, compelling literature, and Nollywood films, Nigeria exports very little to the rest of the world. No one country buys up Nigerian crude oil; buyers vary from year to year, depending on global demand and other market dynamics. The decades-long decline of Nigeria's manufacturing sector means that it is heavily dependent on a wide range of imported goods despite its protectionist trade policies. Looking ahead, international investors and domestic entrepreneurs will deepen Nigeria's ties to the global economy as the country's population grows and its consuming class expands.

Crude oil exports are the foundation of Nigeria's links to the global economy. In 2015 India was the single largest importer of Nigerian crude (20 percent of its exports), followed by The Netherlands, Spain, and Brazil.[26] The United States, in contrast, went from the largest importer of Nigerian oil in 2012 to the tenth largest in 2015 as increased domestic oil production resulting from the "shale boom" squelched demand.[27] Despite being a major oil producer, Nigeria nevertheless imports most of the refined petroleum products it needs—gasoline, kerosene, aviation fuel, and diesel—because officials have mismanaged and embezzled from the country's four state-owned refineries.[28]

Beyond oil, what does Nigeria export? In 2014 it was the world's fourth largest exporter of cocoa beans (cacao) after Cote d'Ivoire, Ghana, and Indonesia, but its production has since stagnated.[29] Nigeria exports roughly 80 percent of its cocoa to Europe.[30] High-quality animal hides from northern Nigeria are much sought after by European and Asian leather makers, which import more than $400 million worth annually.[31]

Spurred on by increasing demand from Asia, Nigeria is the world's sixth largest producer of sesame seeds, a crop that thrives in the poor soil and dry conditions found in north-central Nigeria.[32] Well suited to small-scale farming, sesame cultivation has the potential to improve livelihoods in some of the country's poorest rural areas. Nigeria's non-oil exports are modest for a reason: the one-two punch of the country's multiple oil booms and economic mismanagement by successive governments have greatly narrowed the range and quantity of agricultural commodities and manufactured goods that the country once produced.

Given its large population, Nigeria is a massive market for international consumer and industrial goods. Among global exporters to Nigeria, China unsurprisingly ranks highest, providing 26 percent of its imports in 2014. Of these, electronics, machinery, textiles, construction materials, motorcycles, and vehicle parts top the list. The rising tide of Chinese textile imports, in particular, has had an outsized impact: between 1990 and 2010, the Nigerian textile industry lost more than 100,000 jobs.[33] On the flip side, thousands of Nigerian traders commute between commercial hubs like Lagos and Onitsha and China's manufacturing heartland. Playing an active role in facilitating the flow of exports, Nigerian traders now partner directly with Chinese businesspeople to run factories, warehouses, and export operations.[34]

Looking beyond its trade ties with China, Nigeria imports a huge amount of wheat from the United States. Wheat imports continue to rise, driven by Nigerian consumer demand for bread and the relatively low productivity of the country's nonmechanized, rain-fed wheat farms.[35] Other notable US imports include popular restaurant brands that could be seen as harbingers of Nigeria's growing middle class. Coldstone Creamery, an upscale chain of ice cream shops with hundreds of locations worldwide, is a popular hangout for affluent Lagosians. Pizza mega-brand Domino's also has a foothold in

Nigeria, fusing its Italian American recipes with local flavors in toppings such as chicken suya and jollof rice.[36]

In response to pressure from foreign competitors, Nigerian businesspeople and their political allies have taken to social media with "#MadeInNigeria" and "#BuyNaijaToGrowTheNaira" campaigns aimed at promoting locally made products. Two senators, for example, recently tweeted photographs of themselves test-driving cars manufactured in Nigeria by Innoson Motors, promising to tweak government procurement laws to favor Nigerian products.[37] Similarly, top politicians hailed a Nigerian Army (NA) decision to buy 50,000 pairs of boots made by local shoemakers in southern Nigeria, with one ambitiously proclaiming that "patronage of Made-in-Nigeria goods is an obvious panacea for our economic problems."[38]

Patriotic rhetoric aside, decades of protectionist trade policies have done little to boost domestic manufacturing but have been a boon to monopolists, black marketeers, and corrupt officials. As the former prime minister of Singapore, Lee Kuan Yew, recounted in his autobiography, documenting a 1966 meeting with Nigeria's finance minister, Festus Okotie Eboh:

> He [Okotie Eboh] was going to retire soon, he said. He had done enough for his country and now had to look after his business, a shoe factory. As finance minister, he had imposed a tax on imported shoes so that Nigeria could make shoes. I [was] incredulous. . . . I went to bed that night convinced that they were a different people playing to a different set of rules.[39]

Subsequent governments have continued to experiment with tariffs and import bans. They have hoped that these measures would be a silver bullet, failing to recognize that the decline of indigenous manufacturing and agro-industry was a result of a broader range of factors. Since the country's 1999 return to civilian rule, the government has remained wedded to protectionist trade policies, while at the same time allowing powerful individuals to secure import waivers from the Ministry of Trade or directly from the presidency itself.[40] Critics contend, for example, that one of Nigeria's largest conglomerates, the Dangote Group, owes its profits and dominant market share to decades of protectionist policies and its ties to political leaders.[41] Likewise, a long-standing ban on importing frozen chickens, championed by former president Obasanjo, has raised eyebrows, not least because it benefits the owner of one of the country's largest poultry farms, Obasanjo himself.

What will Nigeria's economy look like in fifteen years?

Nigeria's economic shock absorbers undoubtedly will be put to the test over the next fifteen years, leaving the country in the same predicament it is now: full of promise but bedeviled by oil-driven boom-bust cycles. New technology and international assistance will only somewhat mitigate the strain of climate change, population growth, and rapid urbanization on the economy. In this "business as usual" scenario—as well as in the best and worst case alternative futures—Nigeria's economic trajectory will depend on the quality of governance as well as the scale and scope of elite corruption. The degree to which insecurity, worrying demographic trends, looming environmental shocks, and exogenous influences such as global crude prices negatively impact Nigeria's economic growth and development will also hinge on how well the country is governed.

Best Case Scenario

Following is a description of how a Nigeria in which good governance begets economic growth might look.

After nearly dissolving altogether, a social contract between government officials and citizens re-emerges. Better political leadership and more accountable governance at the federal level and in some states lead to this gradual transformation.

As electoral reforms take root and voters' political awareness grows, elections grow to become a referendum on Nigerians' satisfaction with the performance of politicians and their ability to deliver public goods. Nigerian ministries, agencies, and state governments begin to adopt international transparency, open contracting standards, and management controls. A reformed, more impartial judiciary works to repair its professional reputation. Basic prevention measures and better land use practices mitigate the impact of drought, desertification, soil erosion, and seasonal flooding brought on by climate change.

Nigeria's economy, especially its critically important agricultural sector, develops beyond mere subsistence farming and starts to modernize. Small-scale agro-processing businesses proliferate across rural areas, improving value chains and reducing urban/rural income inequality. Nigeria's booming service sector expands beyond Lagos and attracts significant international investment. Gas flaring and oil spills, ubiquitous in the Niger Delta region, decrease as government, industry, and communities cooperate to curtail them. Nigerians in rural areas adopt newly affordable renewable energy sources in place of diesel generators and charcoal cook stoves. Better federal and state governance increases the overall ease of doing business.

Nigeria's socioeconomic development trajectory brightens as governance, security, environmental, and macroeconomic developments trend positively. Of these, good governance is the most important; Nigeria's socioeconomic progress was long hampered by endemic—and systemic—fraud, waste, and mismanagement by state and local officials notionally responsible for health, education, and individual economic empowerment. Instead of seeing socioeconomic development as a mechanism for self-enrichment, government officials become more responsive to citizens' needs. Nigeria's demographic challenges subside somewhat, especially in the country's deeply impoverished north. After more than a decade of good governance, economic diversification, and unprecedented investment in health and education, demographic pressures begin to wane. Nigeria's overall population growth rate slows from 2.6 percent (in 2015) to a more manageable 2 percent.

Most Likely Scenario

In this "business as usual" scenario, global crude prices gradually rebound, easing the pressure on Nigeria's public finances and reducing its need to borrow. Nigeria retains its status as Africa's largest economy but is unable to break free of boom-bust economic cycles. Despite several years of sustained GDP growth, the country's economic expansion fails to keep pace with population increases. Government efforts to diversify the economy show progress as the country's agricultural, light manufacturing, and information technology sectors expand.

With 263 million people, Nigeria is the fifth most populous country in the world in 2030, just as the UN had predicted in 2015. The share of Nigeria's population under age fifteen increases, exacerbating the country's long-standing "youth bulge." Socioeconomic disparities between northern and southern Nigeria remain stark. Despite an ambitious effort to construct power plants, electricity supply fails to keep pace with growing demand.

The state functions primarily as a public employment mechanism and as a means to distribute oil revenues. Despite periodic anti-kleptocracy drives, corruption remains endemic at all levels of government. At the subnational level, the quality of governance varies significantly between states and individual governors. Local government remains moribund.

Government fails to prepare for the negative effects of climate change. A rise in sea level inundates low-lying neighborhoods in Lagos and forces communities built amid the mangrove swamps in the Niger Delta to relocate. An unusually long drought and the expansion of the Sahara Desert spark southward migration by Sahelian peoples, heightening competition over land and water and increasing the frequency and scope of deadly clashes between farmers and herdsmen.

Worst Case Scenario

What would an unlikely—but possible—worst case scenario for the Nigerian economy look like? Something like this.

A series of badly flawed elections yields successive governments that are little more than criminal enterprises. The modus operandi of senior government officials centers on corruption and abuse of power. Ethnic and religious political fault lines widen. Nigeria becomes an international pariah, as it was under the Abacha regime or as South Sudan is in 2017. While always corruption prone, Nigeria's judiciary and legislature become mere rubber stamps on executive power.

Global crude prices stay stuck below $50 per barrel for over a decade. Nigeria's economy contracts as poor governance and insecurity repel foreign investment and undercut domestic entrepreneurs. National and subnational debt balloons, putting Nigeria at risk of default. Fiscal mismanagement sends the naira into a tailspin, triggering Zimbabwe-like hyperinflation. Once middle-class Nigerians struggle to make ends meet. Large sections of Nigeria's main road arteries become impassable during the rainy season, and some major bridges collapse in disrepair.

Nigerians dependent on subsistence agriculture are unable to cope with fluctuating environmental conditions. Areas of northern Nigeria become virtually uninhabitable, sparking mass migration. Nigerians come to make up the largest share of African migrants making the risky journey to Europe. At the same time, Nigeria experiences a pollution crisis. Aging oil infrastructure, artisanal mines, and unregulated industries dump toxic chemicals into rivers. Due to government failures to invest in clean energy sources, most Nigerians still rely on diesel generators and firewood.

In response to deteriorating socioeconomic conditions, Nigeria's birth rate spikes. As the birth rate climbs above 3 percent, Nigeria is on track to overtake the United States as the third most populated country by 2040—instead of by 2050, as predicted in 2015. Child and maternal mortality rates, particularly in northern Nigeria, worsen as a result of government failure to invest in basic health and sanitation infrastructure.

3

RELIGION

Nigerians like to say that they are the "happiest people in the world and the most religious." Religiosity permeates public life, events big and small are routinely ascribed to divine intervention. Sickness and other misfortunes are the result of spiritual, rather than physical, causes, and many Muslims and Christians eschew modern medicine in favor of faith healing. Evil and witchcraft are countered by miracles and prayer. Virtually all events open and close with a prayer. The visually powerful presence of the National Mosque and the National Church in the capital city of Abuja is aptly symbolic of the importance of religion in Nigerian life.[1] Agnosticism or atheism is not common in Nigeria, nor is lack of faith. While almost all Nigerians are either Christian or Muslim, many still practice traditional beliefs such as magic and ancestor worship. Most Nigerian families are only two or three generations removed from traditional animist and polytheistic beliefs.

What are relations like between the two major religions?

Conflicts between Christians and Muslims receive widespread media attention, even though they may begin as ethnic rivalries or disputes over land and water use, or by politicians seeking to advance their own agendas. The resulting conflicts often acquire religious labels and even coloration. When examined closely, incidents in which Muslim mobs burn down churches in the north and Middle Belt—or where Christian militias attack Fulani herdsmen and Hausa traders—appear to be motivated as much by ethnic and socioeconomic tensions as by religious antipathy. When conflicts are reported in the Nigerian and international media, religion often stands in as a proxy for more complex causes of conflict.

There is a religious revival underway in Nigeria. Among Muslims, there is a renewed focus on making the hajj (pilgrimage to Mecca); returning to the literal meaning of the Koran, known as Salafism; and ridding Islam of non-Koranic elements borrowed from traditional African religion. There is also a growing Iranian-influenced Shia minority that is just a few decades old.

The number of Christians has increased dramatically over the past century. To many Muslims in the north, the explosive growth of Christianity is destabilizing to traditional institutions, particularly the emirate system. The growth owes little to conversion of Muslims. It is instead the result of missionary activity directed at adherents to traditional African religions, from Sierra Leone as well as England (Anglicans), Scotland (Presbyterian), Denmark (Lutheran), and Ireland (Roman Catholic). Furthermore, minority tribes prepared to move from, or add to, their traditional religion have found Christianity more attractive than Islam, especially in the north and the Middle Belt. Christianity is associated with the modern world, while Islam is identified with the trans-Saharan slave trade, which had preyed on "pagans" such as they had been.

Though Anglicanism and Roman Catholicism are commonly believed to be the largest Christian denominations by number of adherents, the Pentecostal and "African" churches appear to be growing the fastest. Among them, there is an emphasis on feeling and emotion ("spirit") rather than on theological concepts. Moreover, Anglican and Roman Catholic parishes are including in their services styles of worship associated with the Pentecostal churches. In general, though with many exceptions, relations are good between the mainstream Christian denominations and the traditional Sufi-influenced Islam of the emirs of northern Nigeria. Salafist Muslims, again with many exceptions, do not have close relations with any of the Christian denominations. Particularly poor are relations between Salafist Islam and the "African" or Pentecostal churches, perhaps because each has a populist and dogmatic outlook and they compete for converts among those who were previously adherents to traditional religion.

Clearly, neither world religion in Nigeria is monolithic. Nigerian Islam, predominantly Sunni in character, has closer historical ties with Islamic centers of learning in Khartoum and Cairo than with those in the Middle East. Africa's Sufi religious brotherhoods play an important role in individual lives, transmitting ideas and facilitating commerce across the entire Sahel, from Khartoum to Dakar. Sufi mystical spirituality has been characterized by broadly tolerant attitudes and the incorporation of certain indigenous African religious practices.

Sufism is anathema to Salafism, a reform movement based on a literal reading of seventh-century holy texts. Salafism was introduced after independence by missionaries from Saudi Arabia and sustained in part by an increase in pilgrimages to Mecca and by social media. Boko Haram is a violent Salafist variant and often accuses traditional Nigerian Sufis of being apostates. Among other things, the conflict between Boko Haram and the more traditional Muslims in the north can be characterized as a civil war within Islam.

In a country where religion is predominant despite the ostensibly secular constitution, religious leaders often are also political leaders and ethnic chieftains. For example, the current vice president of Nigeria, Yemi Osinbajo, is a Pentecostal preacher, a dual-hatting that occasions no particular comment. Within Islam, there is identification of the religious and secular in all aspects of life, including politics. For most Nigerians, the concept of "separation of church and state" is more about maintaining a balance of power between Islam and Christianity rather than an intrinsic belief in secularism.

How religious are Nigerians?

There has never been a nationwide religious census in Nigeria, but it is commonly said that the adherents of each world religion number about half of the population, and that Nigeria is by far the largest country in the world in which neither Christians nor Muslims are a minority.[2]

Former military head of state Murtala Muhammed (1975–1976) famously voiced this fifty-fifty formula as conventional wisdom. Although that idea is politically convenient, it is not necessarily accurate. Muslims in the north have a much higher birth rate than Christians nationwide, and thus Muslims may slightly outnumber Christians nationally. More important, however, is that Christians dominate the modern economy and the media and enjoy better access to education than Muslims.[3] Hence, Christians tend to be more prominent in public life. Moreover, they are also heavily represented in the Nigerian diaspora in Europe and the United States. With Nigerian Christians' economic and cultural domination in the country and large presence overseas, many Nigerians perceive Nigeria as a majority-Christian nation.

Underpinning these faiths, both of which come from outside of Africa, is a substratum of traditional African religion that often influences individual behavior, including the practice of magic and ancestor worship. For example, 11 percent of Nigerians believe that sacrifice to spirits or ancestors can protect them from misfortune, a belief condemned by Christianity and Islam.[4] Many Nigerians' beliefs rest on a continuum, with traditional religion at one end and sophisticated forms of Islam or Christianity at the other. Some ethnic groups, notably the Yoruba, identify with a specific pantheon of gods. These vary in size and sophistication, but they generally have in common the control of the natural world. Adherents of traditional religion and those of Christianity and Islam will often be believers in magic and witchcraft. This coexistence—or fusion—of traditional and Muslim and/or Christian religious beliefs is known as syncretism.

Occultist practices, based on African traditional religion, persist beneath the surface among Christians and Muslims. Some are associated with premodern burial practices, and in rare cases, with ritual killing and cannibalism. Mob killing of witches continues, and though it is treated as murder by the secular state, prosecution is rare. Politicians play a significant role in perpetuating the occult, leveraging it to advance their own agendas.

Traditional religion is strong enough that devout Muslims and Christians are fearful and suspicious of it. They see it as dangerous, not picturesque or folkloric. Nigerians are often embarrassed by its persistence, especially in their interactions with non-Nigerians. Some will not display tribal masks and other items associated with traditional worship, even if only as works of art. The need to hold "paganism" at bay probably contributes to the authoritarianism, theological fundamentalism, and lack of questioning characteristic of much of popular Christianity and Islam in Nigeria. The view that apostates from Islam must die is widespread among Nigerian Muslims in the north, although not elsewhere. It is based on a literal reading of the Koran and seventh-century religious writing that was particularly hostile to "paganism."

Christian and Muslim religious rhetoric is often triumphalist, with claims that a particular brotherhood, congregation, or fellowship is the biggest and the best. Among Christian adherents to the "prosperity" gospel, individual wealth is seen as evidence of God's special favor. Both religions have an "edifice complex," a proclivity for building large houses of worship. Muslims benefit from many large, well-equipped mosques, often built by Saudi missionary societies.

Nigerian Christians have built many megachurches, some with funding from evangelical Christian groups in the United

States. How much money has been contributed is impossible to know; Americans are free to donate to any cause they like, and there are no US-imposed exchange controls on cash transfers to Nigeria. One church, Prayer City, says it can host 200,000 worshippers at a time. Nigerians maintain that their Christianity, as represented by their mainline churches, is more "authentic" than that in the West. Similarly, Nigerian Muslims argue that Islam has been present in Africa for more than a millennium and has little to learn from the Middle East.

Nigeria's National Mosque and the National Church dominate Abuja's skyline. The former is conventional in style and was heavily supported by Saudi charities. It was completed in 1984 and was one of the first monumental buildings constructed in Abuja. The latter is a superb, original work of architecture by Darchiwork Group, based in Lagos. It was completed more than twenty years after the National Mosque, in 2005. Then president Obasanjo was treasurer of the completion committee. It was consecrated as an Anglican cathedral by the Anglican primate at the time in his capacity as chairman of the nondenominational Christian Association of Nigeria (CAN). It is used for services marking national events and does not belong to any particular denomination.

Both Muslims and Christians in Nigeria are strongly opposed to gay rights. As in Uganda, in Nigeria homosexual activity—or even supporting organizations advocating for LGBT rights—may be punished by ten to fourteen years in prison. However, prosecutions appear to be rare, and the Nigerian media have not reported any such sentences as having been carried out. There are anecdotes about extrajudicial violence against homosexuals, but it is unclear how extensive it is.

Does Nigeria have a dominant religion, and how do its different faiths interact?

As discussed previously, the official consensus is that Christians and Muslims each make up about half of the population. So neither is a minority, but neither is predominant. That consensus drives government policy. The federal government makes every effort to balance the interests of the two faiths and to show favor to neither. However, zealots from both religions regularly claim that the government favors the other.

Neither religion is dominant over the other, but religion is dominant over secularism. Despite the ostensibly secular nature of the federal government, all levels of governance accord religion a significant role, reflecting the outlook of almost all Nigerians. The military, on the other hand, is much more secular in outlook. Officers' clubs serve alcoholic beverages even in the predominantly Muslim north, as is permitted by federal law, if not sharia. Military chiefs of state normally wear their uniforms in public rather than traditional dress that would indicate their ethnicity. Nevertheless, the government sponsors pilgrimages at public expense to Mecca (the hajj) through the National Hajj Commission, and to Jerusalem and other holy sites for Christians through the Nigerian Christian Pilgrimage Commission. There are far more Muslim than Christian pilgrims. In 2016 the Christian Pilgrimage Commission anticipated it would support twenty thousand pilgrims for the whole year, whereas through the Hajj Commission, that same number traveled to Mecca in a single week in 2017.[5] Under Nigeria's federal system, states regularly favor the predominant religion within their borders. For example, Christians bitterly complain that state and local authorities in the north deny them the necessary permits for building churches and for preaching in public spaces, while in the south minority complaints more often involve discrimination based on ethnicity rather than religion.

From an outsider's perspective, Nigeria's Muslims and Christians have similar views on many social issues. For both, the individual owes his or her highest loyalty first to family, then religion, and then to ethnic group, while the state comes up last. Both respect elders, and both, in their own way, establish a separate, usually subordinate, space for women. With respect to children, the father's rights are superior to those of the mother. For most Nigerian Christians and Muslims, the Western concept of a rigid separation between religious and secular spheres is incompatible with "true religion."

Islam has been present in Nigeria for more than a thousand years, far longer than Christianity, for which a significant presence only dates back to the nineteenth century. The identification of Sunni and Shia, so important in the Middle East, played a negligible role in Nigerian Islam before the later part of the twentieth century, when Sunni and Salafist identity was promoted by Saudi Sunni missionary societies and Shia by equivalent Iranian groups.

A few American missionaries have also been active, notably Jehovah's Witnesses and the Church of Jesus Christ of Latter-day Saints (Mormons). Nigerian media refer to the Jehovah's Witnesses as numbering in the "millions," surely an exaggeration. However, they are more numerous than Mormons, who officially estimate their numbers at more than 150,000. Converts to both churches appear to come from other Christian denominations rather than from the traditional religions or Islam. Mormon growth dates from 1978, when that church first admitted blacks to the priesthood. Jehovah's Witnesses, first established at the end of the nineteenth century, are known for their educational institutions. Both are strongly influenced by their American mother churches.

Reflecting their interpretation of seventh-century holy texts, many Muslims in the north and the Middle Belt regard converting to Christianity as worthy of death. On the other hand, especially in the Yoruba southwest, individuals move back and forth between Christianity and Islam with relative ease. Former president Obasanjo, a Yoruba born-again Baptist, refers favorably to his Muslim sister in public, and he keeps both the Lenten and Ramadan fasts. Nevertheless, Presidents Obasanjo and Jonathan cultivated evangelical and Pentecostal Christians as part of their political base. Secularism in Nigeria remains weak.

How has Islam in Nigeria been changing?

Islam in Nigeria is highly diverse. In the north, Islam is historically associated with the Sultanate of Sokoto, the shehu of Borno, and their subordinate emirates. For most of these Muslims, religious and government authority is fused. Elsewhere, notably in the southwest around Lagos, Muslims acknowledge the difference between the secular and religious spheres and are more supportive of the concept of a secular state. The Middle Belt is a borderland between ethnicities, as well as between Islam and Christianity. It is populated by many small ethnic groups, a handful of small emirates, and a large population of Christians (albeit one that is still probably a minority in the area). This mix makes the region a venue for clashes that often have a religious dimension imputed to them but also reflect differences and rivalries over land and water use and ethnicity.

The Nigerian Supreme Council for Islamic Affairs (NSCIA) is the most important coordinating body for Muslims. For example, it determines the beginning and end of the holy season of Ramadan through its authoritative sightings of the moon, and it represents Muslim, primarily Sunni, interests to federal and state governments. The sultan of Sokoto heads NSCIA. For many years its general secretary was Lagos lawyer Lateef Adegbite, a skilled intermediary between Muslims, the secular government, and Christian groups.

Islam in northern Nigeria has been characterized by periodic waves of reform justified as a means to purify society by establishing justice for the poor. As we have seen, strict implementation of sharia law without distinction between poor and rich—or strong and weak—has been a persistent element in these reform movements. On the other hand, in the southwest states there has been little serious agitation for the adoption of sharia in the criminal domain. Seventy-one percent of Muslims in Nigeria would like sharia to be the official law of the land; among Muslims in sub-saharan Africa, the figure is slightly lower, 64 percent.[6]

In the north, continuity among the precolonial, colonial, and post-independence systems of governance and society more generally is stronger than elsewhere in Nigeria. In the period immediately preceding the beginning of British colonization, the 1806 jihad led by Usman Dan Fodio established the Sultanate of Sokoto. Dan Fodio conquered most of what is now northern Nigeria, with the notable exception of the Kingdom of Bornu, which was able to preserve its independence and its indigenous ruler, the shehu. With more than a thousand years of history, the Kingdom of Bornu is one of Africa's most ancient Islamic empires. Late in the nineteenth century its territory was divided among the British (Nigeria), French (Niger), and Germans (Kamerun, now Cameroon). The state of Borno in today's Nigeria consists only of the British share of that division. The family of the current shehu came to the throne in the early nineteenth century, about the same time that Dan Fodio was active, and as with the sultan of Sokoto, his position was largely preserved by the British under their policy of indirect rule. Ethnically, the Sultanate of Sokoto consisted of a Fulani ruling class and mostly Hausa subjects. The area that was once the Kingdom of Bornu remains ethnically Kanuri and Kanuri-speaking. Some observers see Boko Haram as predominantly Kanuri, but this is disputed. Others argue that although in its early days Kanuri ethnicity comprised the majority of the movement, now Boko Haram draws supporters from all over the north.

Under Dan Fodio's successors, Sokoto became a sophisticated and successful Islamic state based on the trans-Saharan slave trade. After abolishing slavery and eliminating some of the penology of sharia that they regarded as cruel, the British largely left the emirate institutions in place. Sharia remained the legal code for Muslims, but it operated in parallel with British jurisprudence. Hence, there is significant social and religious continuity between modern northern Nigeria and the two Muslim kingdoms, the Sultanate of Sokoto and the Kingdom of Bornu. The British successfully co-opted the traditional

Islamic leadership in the north, as has their successor, the secular state based in Abuja.

Radical Islamic movements, in their present form, are relatively new to Nigeria. They date from the post-independence period and became vehicles for popular protest against the bad governance characteristic of northern Nigeria and the growing impoverishment of a population that was already one of the poorest in the Muslim world. In the southwest, social protest is more commonly channeled by Yoruba cultural movements, rather than by radical Islamic ones.

In the recent past, Salafist—and, to a lesser extent, Shia—reform movements in the north have taken hold. Salafism emphasizes the literal reading of the Koran and some seventh-century texts. As a practical matter, the Sunni–Shia dichotomy reached significance in Nigeria only after the Iranian Revolution in 1979 and reflects the increasing incorporation of northern Nigerian Islam into the modern Muslim world.

"Reformist" movements have included Izala, Maitatsine, Darul Islam, and Boko Haram most recently. While there are numerous differences among them, all look to establish an Islamic polity conducted according to sharia. In general, they reject the West and modern science in all of its forms. At differing times, many have been associated with violence. Salafist and Shia reform movements enjoy support among the poor but also attract high school graduates and university students. Their founders are usually outsized personalities. For example, Mohammed Yusuf and Ibrahim El Zakzaky, respectively the founders of Boko Haram and the Shia Islamic Movement of Nigeria (IMN), were both dynamic and charismatic preachers.

Islam in northern Nigeria, in both its moderate and radical forms, is sustained by a network of Koranic schools, which enroll more than ten million students. The curriculum is centered on the memorization of the Koran and other holy texts. Little, if any, of the Western curriculum, including subjects like English or mathematics, is included. These schools have grown explosively. As agriculture in the north has declined, rural families have sent their children to Koranic schools in the cities, where they beg in the mornings, study in the afternoons, and, most importantly, eat. More secular Nigerian observers are critical of the Koranic schools because they do not prepare their students to participate in the modern economy. They are part of the context out of which radical, jihadist movements emerge, although they are generally not violent. There is push-back against these schools in the north, and certain governors are looking for ways to introduce modern subjects, such as mathematics and English, into the curriculum.

Radical movements have made little headway in the south-west of the country, dominated by the Yoruba and home to the great metropolitan centers of Lagos and Ibadan. Yoruba Muslims freely intermarry with Christians and cheerfully in-corporate elements of traditional Yoruba religion into their own. Once of little relevance, the distinctions between Salafist and Shia appear to be growing in terms of self-identification. Yoruba Muslims are relatively outward looking, owing to their urbanization and longer exposure to the West. Unlike in the north, Yoruba Muslims are fully invested in the secular state.

What makes Nigerian Christianity unique?

Nigerian Christianity is dynamic, and its following is growing rapidly, especially among the evangelical, charismatic, and Pentecostal churches, memberships of which frequently overlap. This growth is so significant that the styles of worship of Pentecostal churches are now influencing the Anglican and Roman Catholic churches. In general Pentacostal styles of worship (outside specifically Pentacostal denominations) in-fluence Protestants to a greater degree than Roman Catholics: a Pew Forum survey showed that six in ten Protestants were Pentecostal or charismatic in style of worship, while only three in ten Roman Catholics were.[7] A number of Pentecostal churches in Nigeria have close ties to the United States. In addition, there are numerous other churches, which some-times incorporate elements from African traditional religion, such as permitting multiple wives.

Often grouped together as *aladura* (the Yoruba word for "praying"), these churches are independent of other structures and are often led by a charismatic "prophet." Most Christians, whatever their denomination, tend to be new to the religion; they are either converts, usually from traditional religion, or their parents or grandparents were. Compared to Western Christians, those in Nigeria are fervent and at the same time authoritarian, rule-based, emotional, and have little tolerance for ambiguity or doubt. Many are biblical literalists.

Despite the popularity of Pentecostal churches, Anglican and Roman Catholic churches still boast large followings. Anglicans number more than twenty million, and the number of Roman Catholics is most likely slightly higher. (For comparison, in the United States about 72 million people identify themselves as Roman Catholic, and in the UK, about 27 million identify as Anglican.) The two churches together include roughly half of all the Christians in Nigeria. Highly conservative by Western social standards, Nigerian Anglicans and Roman Catholics are often homophobic and strongly opposed to gay marriage and—among Roman Catholics—divorce. Some Nigerian Anglican bishops have encouraged American congregations to break away from the Episcopal Church because of the ordination by the latter of women and gays in the priesthood. Yet supranational identity is still of great importance to most Anglicans and Roman Catholics, illustrated by Nigerian Anglicans' formal title, "the Church of Nigeria–Anglican Communion." Nigerian Catholic politicians often ignore Rome's teaching, especially on social justice and alleviation of poverty, yet fervently proclaim their loyalty to the pope.

During the colonial and early independence period, Christian churches founded and operated schools and hospitals, often of high quality. The military government "nationalized" such institutions in the aftermath of the civil war, leading to a dramatic decline in quality. However, after the restoration of civilian government in 1999, President Olusegun Obasanjo relinquished the state's monopoly on education, allowing for the establishment of new schools and universities, many by Christian denominations. However, the state has not returned former Christian institutions to their founders.

The seminary with the largest enrollment in the Roman Catholic Church worldwide is said to be Bigard Memorial, in Enugu, which is in Igboland. Established in its present form only in 1978, it has produced three cardinals, eleven archbishops, and thirty-one bishops. Pentecostal and charismatic Nigerian churches have established congregations beyond Africa; most large American cities host several. Initially serving the religious needs of African immigrants, they are expanding their reach to native-born Americans.

Many Nigerian Christian leaders are highly critical of the social norms in the West, and they often seek to reform their mother churches. They object to Western "relativism" with respect to Christian doctrine. Flashpoints are the evolving Western views on the equality of women and rights of gay, lesbian, and transgender people, which many in Nigeria see as contrary to the teachings of the Bible and disruptive to the "natural" social order. With declining clergy vocations in the developed world, Nigeria exports significant numbers of clergy to fill this void. They are often advocates of a more traditional form of Christianity than they find in their new homes. Nigerian Anglican and Roman Catholic bishops try to discourage this exodus of clergy to the developed world, a movement that is similar to the outmigration underway among other professions, notably medicine, where Western demand is strong.

The Christian Association of Nigeria (CAN) is the primary arm of political action for most Christian denominations. In 2016 Olasupo Ayokunle, head of the Nigerian Baptist Convention, began a three-year term as CAN president.

Organized in 1976, CAN initially included only the Anglican, Roman Catholic, and other "mainstream" churches. It has since steadily broadened its membership and now includes Pentecostal, charismatic, and African Aladura churches. Its consistent theme has been opposition to sharia law. Its leadership has used rhetoric hostile to Islam, and it has been accused of fomenting interfaith violence. At times, CAN supports specific presidential candidates, which can create fissures within the organization. For example, in 2014 the Roman Catholic hierarchy withdrew from CAN at the national level because it felt the organization was tying itself too closely to President Jonathan.

Though there is considerable variation from one part of the country to another, Christians and Muslims tend to view each other with suspicion. Where religious boundaries coincide with those of ethnicity and land use, conflict can be frequent and intense, as it is in parts of the Middle Belt. There, Muslim Fulani herdsmen overlap with predominantly Christian farmers from many different ethnic groups, and it is unclear whether the killings are the result of religion, ethnicity, or land use. However, there are people, particularly among the elite, who advocate for more unity, arguing that Christians and Muslims together are "peoples of the book"; that is, they share the same holy scriptures and are both "children of Abraham." For many elites, this overarching unity between the two religions should banish religious conflict. However, such views are much less common among ordinary people in the street. Outbursts of religious violence very often have a populist, antiestablishment dimension.

4

POLITICS

NIGERIA'S GREAT GAME

Under its current constitution, Nigeria is a federal republic. Executive, legislative, and judicial powers at the national and state levels, as well as state and local authorities, have some autonomy and many responsibilities. Government at all levels is—in theory—supposed to be directly responsible to the people. The president and vice president, as well as senators and representatives in the National Assembly, are directly elected by popular vote nationwide.

The same pattern is followed in the thirty-six state governments, each of which has a governor and a state assembly, except for Abuja and the Federal Capital Territory, which is governed by a dedicated federal ministry. Nigeria is nominally democratic, but many Nigerians vote at the direction of local elites on whom they are dependent, rather than making informed choices about individual candidates.

A fundamental principle of governance enshrined in Nigeria's 1999 constitution is "federal character," which mandates that government appointments and revenue at all levels are to be distributed equitably throughout the country. A common practice is for the administration in Abuja to award one minister and one minister of state to each of the thirty-six states. Ambassadorial as well as senior military and police officer appointments are also supposed to be distributed equitably across the federation. At local and state levels, offices and other public resources are distributed among ethnic and sometimes even religious groups. Following federal character rules to the letter can be cumbersome, resulting in cabinets that are so large as to be unwieldy and the appointment of officials whose only apparent qualification is their state of origin. Nevertheless, in a country so fractured by ethnicity, religion, and regionalism, federal character has been an important mechanism for keeping the country together.

Beyond federal character rules, the principle of power and resource sharing is deeply ingrained in Nigerian politics. One important means of achieving this is through the informal practice of "zoning": distributing political offices among ethnogeographic zones at the federal, state, and even local levels. Many Nigerians believe, for example, that the presidency should alternate between the largely Muslim north and the mostly Christian south, even though it has rarely done so. At the state level, Nigerians expect the governorship to rotate among each state's three senatorial districts and for the governor, deputy governor, and speaker of the state legislature to each represent one of these districts. Even though zoning is not part of the constitution as federal character is, it is a common practice in the country's two major political parties.

Politics is more important in Nigeria than in the United States or in Western Europe because there are few other alternatives for elite competition or enrichment. Personal wealth is largely accrued by gaining access to the oil and gas sectors, which are controlled by the state. All production is through joint ventures or agreements between the national oil company and private companies, both domestic and foreign. Finance, banking, real estate, telecommunications, and the stock market are ultimately driven by petrochemical production. Wealth creation runs through the oil and gas sector via the government.

In Nigeria, politics is the means by which competing and cooperating elites divide up the country's wealth ("the national cake"). Compensation for public office holders is exceptionally generous. Members of the National Assembly, for example, receive more than $1 million per year for salary and operating expenses. Individual members are subject to no oversight in how they use these funds. By comparison, US legislators earn $174,000 per year, and while they also enjoy additional funds for operating expenses, these must be used for specific purposes, must be accounted for, and are rigidly controlled. In addition, in Nigeria legislators often have privileged access to government contracts. Therefore, it should come as no surprise that the surest way to riches and power is through elected office and the opportunities for kleptocratic state capture that it offers. That makes politics, in the words of former president Obasanjo, "a do-or-die affair."

Nigerian political institutions historically have been weak, in part because politics has been based on patronage and clientage networks, not formal political institutions, processes, or policy initiatives. This "prebendal" system—referring to the medieval European practice of granting official positions as political rewards—was first labeled as such by Richard Joseph three decades ago.[1] However, the restoration of civilian governance in 1999, the succession of a civilian president after another civilian in 2007, and the credible election of an opposition leader in 2015 are strong indications of changes to come. While politics continues to be an elite game largely played without reference to the Nigerian people, Nigeria's trajectory is toward democracy.

How does Nigeria's federal system work?

The federal government is responsible for security at all levels, international relations, economic policy and development strategies, the hydrocarbon industry, the implementation of justice, the currency, most taxation, and much else. All oil and gas is the property of the federal government, as is the national territory. (Land use rights may be bought and sold, not the land itself.) The federal and state governments have shared authority over education and health, while local governments are involved in day-to-day, small-scale administration, such as regulating markets. The security services (including the police) are federal and answer to the president; there are no state or local police forces. In addition, there are quasi-legal vigilante groups, notably the Civilian Joint Task Force (CJTF), which is involved in the struggle against Boko Haram, and the *hisbah,* a group that enforces sharia criminal law among Muslims.

Nigeria's 1999 constitution was strongly influenced by that of the United States. But an important difference is that a military government imposed the country's constitution, without any process of popular ratification. Successive military governments created Nigeria's current array of states in a top-down process in which residual powers remained at the center. The US Constitution, though also drafted by elites, went through a process of wider popular ratification. Furthermore, the US states created the federal government, and they retain residual powers. In comparison, in Nigeria the reality is that power is much more concentrated in the presidency and among the governors than a reading of the constitution would indicate.

Nigerian federalism is quite flawed and more aspirational than real in many ways. In practice it reflects Nigeria's social and economic organization into competing patronage/clientage networks and the concentration of power in the presidency and among the governors, a characteristic of other oil states. Power flows from the top down, from the patron to the client, not from the bottom up. Hence, state governors may be part of the president's network, while state assembly members may be part of the governor's network, which ultimately makes them part of the president's network. A rival network to the president's might be headed by a senator in the National Assembly and could include one or more state governors. A state governor, in turn, is likely to have personal ties with members of his state assembly. Assembly members may have close ties with local government authorities where they are not altogether moribund. Many rival patron and client combinations usually exist and are in flux. But the president in theory has sole control of the state's coercive capacity through the military and the police. Top-down governance dominated by elite horse-trading is profoundly conservative and self-regarding. The people of Nigeria are largely detached from the process. This detachment also accounts in part for the slow development of a sense of national identity.

Federal revenue, more than 70 percent of which comes from oil and gas when markets are stable, is held in the Federation Account.[2] The federal government distributes revenue to the states and local authorities using a formula that is approved by the National Assembly. The Revenue Mobilization Allocation and Fiscal Commission, an autonomous body, provides technical guidance. As required by law, 56 percent of the revenue went to the federal government, 24 percent to the states, and 20 percent to the local government authorities in 2016. This figure tends to vary slightly monthly and annually. Governors are supposed to distribute state-generated revenue to local authorities, also according to a formula. In fact, mechanisms for holding governors accountable for their state expenditure and their distribution of funds to local government authorities are weak. State assemblies are supposed to exercise oversight functions but are frequently in the pocket of the governor. The typical state legislature is a weak institution beholden to the state governor and therefore reluctant to hold him accountable. Hence governors, like the president, are very powerful because of their privileged access to petroleum revenues. As elsewhere, money in Nigeria means power.

As previously mentioned, Nigeria's constitution mandates that the federal government and its operations adhere to the principle of federal character. That is, there may be "no predominance of persons" from a few states or from a few ethnic groups in the government. By extension, the policy dictates that oil revenue be shared with all the states, not just those that produce hydrocarbons. This principle is designed to promote national unity and to be "fair." Proposals to changes in the formula for revenue distribution are highly contentious and are regularly debated in the National Assembly. No consensus has emerged. The oil- and gas-producing states object that their share according to the formula is too small and "unfair," especially given the industry's environmental depredations. In fact, the oil-producing states do receive a premium ("derivation") payment equal to 13 percent of the petroleum revenue generated there. But without exception, oil-producing states want a higher derivation, a demand resisted by many other states in the federation. Dissatisfaction with the distribution of oil revenue is a major driver of militancy in Nigeria's oil patch.

How powerful is Nigeria's president?

Since 1979 Nigeria's federal system has deliberately followed the American constitutional model. As in the United States, Nigeria's president is both head of state and head of government, in theory with powers limited by the constitution and the rule of law, an independent legislature and judiciary, and state and local prerogatives and responsibilities.

However, chiefs of state in Nigeria are often more similar to "big men" in other African countries than to American presidents. Rival elite networks select presidential and gubernatorial candidates through a process of horse-trading within and among the two largest political parties, at present the governing All Progressives Congress (APC) and the People's Democratic Party (PDP). Elections ratify those choices, often through competitive rigging. The nominating and electoral process may be violent when elites fail to reach a consensus on rival candidates, especially at lower levels.

At the conclusion of the electoral process, the Nigerian president is freer of constraints than any American president could ever be. Neither the National Assembly nor the judiciary has been institutionally or politically strong enough to hold the president accountable, except on rare occasions. The effective power of the Nigerian president is greater than the constitution provides for, in part because he has direct access to oil revenue that is often "off the books," in part because he is inevitably the head of an important patron/client network of his own, and in part because most presidents have had close ties to the military, the country's most important national institution. It is notable that President Shehu Shagari (1979–1983) lacked a strong patron/client network and close ties to the military. Accordingly, his presidency was widely regarded as a failure, and he was overthrown by a military coup. This coup was precipitated by elections with competitive rigging so violent that the military stepped in to "punish" the civilian politicians.

Since the restoration of civilian government in 1999, the more usual pattern has been that with all but unlimited access to oil revenue, the president is the most powerful patron of all within Nigeria's complex network of patron/client relationships. Incumbency is a powerful advantage. Nigeria's legislative and judicial branches rarely challenge presidential power. Nor do voters challenge it. Far from being independent, most Nigerian voters are part of, and manipulated by, the patronage/clientage networks that organize society from top to bottom. Instead, a president's power is exercised and limited by rival patron/client networks. The president's power is usually the strongest, but not absolute. Moreover, the 2015 defeat of an incumbent president for the first time by the opposition candidate in credible elections is a sign that the electorate, in tandem with some of the political elite, is moving toward holding the chief of state accountable.

Though largely free of institutional constraints, a fundamental limitation on Nigerian presidential power is the lack of state capacity. The offices and ministries by which a president can impose his will are in many cases weak. Transmission belts between the president and other parts of the government are underdeveloped. The civil service is bloated and ineffective. Even under the military, Nigeria never became a police state because it was not strong enough bureaucratically to do so. Presidential directions and policy initiatives all too frequently remain a dead letter. Future Nigerian chiefs of state may be even weaker than their predecessors, especially if petroleum revenues remain flat or even decline.

Are there checks and balances on presidential power?

In theory, the constitution, the National Assembly, and Nigeria's independent judiciary limit presidential power. But in effect there are few institutional constraints on it. The security services, the military, and the police are directly under presidential authority; there are no state or local police forces in Nigeria, and the president is the commander-in-chief of the armed forces. Usually, the president's patronage/clientage network is strong enough to ensure that his political party is the largest in the National Assembly.

That said, Nigerian presidents cannot function as tyrants accountable to no one but themselves. During the generation of military government, the head of state was the head of a governing committee of senior military officers known as the Armed Forces Ruling Council (or a similar name). Under civilian government, any president's power is limited by the strength of the other elite networks, especially when they are united by consensus. Hence, when the elites came together in 2006, they were strong enough to prevent President Obasanjo

Figure 4.1 Goodluck Ebele Jonathan, president from 2010 to 2015. (Credit: World Economic Forum)

from seeking a third presidential term. They were also strong enough to ensure President Buhari's 2015 electoral victory when they reached a consensus that President Jonathan had to go. (See figures 4.1 and 4.2.)

As we have seen, presidential power is also limited by the lack of bureaucratic and administrative capacity. The Nigerian equivalent of the US Executive Office of the President or the National Security Council is weak and underdeveloped. The Nigerian military appears to have weakened under presidents Jonathan and Buhari, though Buhari has said he will restore Nigeria's military strength.

On the other hand, the ability of the National Assembly, the judiciary, state governments, and local authorities to check presidential power is compromised by the inability of those

Figure 4.2 Muhammadu Buhari, military head of state from 1984 to 1985 and civilian president from 2015 to date. (Credit: US Department of State)

entities to raise revenue on their own. Only Lagos State, of the thirty-six, is able to meet a significant part of its costs using locally generated tax revenue. Otherwise, entities of government ultimately are dependent on revenue from oil and gas controlled and distributed by the federal government and ultimately by the president. Most institutions of government rely on presidential intervention to ensure they are funded sufficiently.

Separation of powers inherently limits a president, and that principle is becoming more real and less aspirational. Prior to the Yar'Adua administration (2007–2010), President Obasanjo violated the constitution without penalty when he declined to enforce certain Supreme Court rulings, riding roughshod over the privileges and prerogatives of the National Assembly and the states. Under Obasanjo, the National Assembly made repeated efforts to impeach him. All failed. However, President Yar'Adua established the principle that the executive is bound to enforce court rulings, and under Presidents Jonathan and Buhari the National Assembly has become increasingly assertive of its constitutional right to review, alter, and approve the national budget.

How do regional and ethnic identities shape Nigerian politics?

An artificial creation of the British Empire that united hundreds of ethnic groups never before incorporated into the same state, Nigeria lacked national politics in the late colonial and early independence eras. Instead of forging a national identity, the country's pioneer politicians primarily sought to advance the interests of themselves, their families, and their particular ethnic groups. The principal political figures of the late colonial and early independence eras came from the three largest ethnic blocs: the Hausa-Fulani, the Yoruba, and the Igbo. Yet these "big three" ethnic groupings together constitute only a little more than half of the country's population, leaving many smaller ethnic groups aggrieved at their seeming exclusion from politics at the highest levels and therefore access to petroleum revenues.

Alienated by mass killings and political marginalization, the predominantly Christian Igbo tried but failed to establish the independent state of Biafra, resulting in the 1967–1970 Nigerian Civil War. In the aftermath a rough, elite consensus emerged that ethnic politicking must never again lead to civil war. The Igbo were superficially reincorporated into national life, but there remains a sense that a post-Biafra "glass ceiling" still exists, preventing the Igbo from holding the presidency. Igbo yearning after an independent state continues to be a factor in the politics of the core territories that once constituted Biafra.

Under civilian president Shagari (1979–1983) politics continued to be regionally and ethnically based. After the overthrow of the Shagari government by a military coup and during the generation of rule by generals and the Armed Forces Ruling Council that followed, military and civilian elites worked to create formal political institutions that would supersede ethnicity and regionalism. Political parties were to be national in scope, not instruments to advance the interests of particular ethnic or religious groups. Hence during the "transition to democracy," military head of state Ibrahim Badamasi Babangida (1985–1993) famously established two political parties, "one slightly to the left, the other slightly to the right."

These parties were military creations largely lacking organic roots among the electorate. Though their names, structures, and leadership have evolved, two large parties endure to this day. For many or most voters, ethnic and religious issues were of greater importance. But such issues were allowed no formal political expression. Hence, political parties were largely irrelevant to most Nigerians. For elites, however, they were the venue for cooperation and competition, for negotiations over how to share the "national cake."

The pattern of formal governance that did not recognize ethnicity and religion despite their central role in the lives of most Nigerians continued after the 1999 restoration of civilian rule. The elites resurrected Babangida's two political parties: the PDP, which dominated politics from 1999 to 2015, and the opposition APC, which is a shifting, elite coalition that has frequently changed its name. Both political parties were essentially elite patronage machines for capturing the state, with little or no focus on policy or issues.

However, both parties are national in scope, and as venues for elite political bargaining they have contributed to a more nationally focused elite outlook. As such, they are a factor in Nigeria's avoiding a renewed civil war. Among the elites, there is an informal understanding that high office and access to privileges rotate among the principal ethnic groups. This reality has promoted political stability. But religion, ethnicity, and regional competition continue to have no formal political expression at the national level. In the north this reality has encouraged the emergence of radical jihadism and hostility to the secular state.

Moreover, after 1999 and the restoration of civilian governance, governors in twelve northern states sponsored the expansion of sharia law to include not just civil cases, but also the criminal domain. Enthusiastic crowds greeted this move as a harbinger of greater justice for the poor. However, neither political party addressed the sharia issue at the national level. In fact the introduction of sharia law in criminal cases involving Muslims changed little and did not improve the delivery of justice for the poor. That reality contributed to greater disillusionment with institutions of government in the north. The perceived failure of governance contributed to the growth of radical forms of Islam, out of which emerged Boko Haram and other similar (if largely nonviolent) movements.

In spite of national political structures, ethnic and religious identities are reinforced by political concepts of "indigeneity." It is an individual's family "state of origin" rather than his or her own, personal "state of residence" that is supposed to determine the venue of that person's political activity. Indigenes have privileges that those of outside origin do not; especially with respect to local and state authorities, not all Nigerians are equal. Even after being resident for several generations, it is difficult for non-natives to obtain government-issued certificates of indigeneity. For example, in Plateau State Muslim Fulani herdsmen and Hausa traders have their historic origin outside the state; Christian Berom farmers are indigenes. Many Hausa and Fulani are blocked from voting in state and local elections. However, ethnic Berom can do so freely, guaranteeing that the state government is Christian dominated and champions the interests of the Berom and other indigenous ethnic groups. As a result, notions of indigeneity fuel ethnic and religious conflict in Plateau State.

Indigeneity and the effort to enforce it are open to political abuse and manipulation. Some politicians in the Middle Belt are notorious for using it to stack the deck against their political opponents and to whip up the support of their fellow indigenes. Manipulation of indigeneity during tense election periods, especially where elites are divided, can be a significant driver of violence. But even in peaceful parts of the country, the concept of indigencity retards the development of a common sense of Nigerian national identity.

Why do state governors matter?

Even though the president and other federal officials exercise great sway over national affairs, Nigeria's thirty-six state governors arguably exercise more influence over the country's overall stability, economic prosperity, and social welfare. Nigeria's international partners and foreign investors often overestimate the on the-ground influence of national elites when seeking to facilitate a business deal or help tackle insecurity and promote good governance.

Both national power brokers and local party kingpins, governors sit atop the political food chain in their respective states, each with a population, economic profile, and budget on a par with that of a small to medium-sized country (see table 4.1). By no means bit players, state governors have made decisions over the years that caused global oil prices to fluctuate, fueled the rise of Boko Haram, and arrested the spread of Ebola to Nigeria. They also act informally as state sheriffs, often ameliorating—though sometimes aggravating—local security conditions.

Nigerian state governors are more powerful than their American counterparts, propelling presidents, ministers,

Table 4.1 Select Nigerian States and Countries with Comparable Populations

State	2017 Population (Est.)	Comparable Country
Kano	13,411,000	South Sudan
Lagos	12,746,000	Rwanda
Kaduna	8,398,000	Switzerland
Oyo	8,077,000	Papua New Guinea
Katsina	8,018,000	Israel
Rivers	7,490,000	Bulgaria
Bauchi	6,755,000	Laos
Borno	5,997,000	Denmark
Jigawa	5,956,000	Lebanon
Benue	5,840,000	Singapore

Source: Population Reference Bureau, World Population Data Sheet, 2017 (http://www.prb.org); Gates Foundation Vaccination Tracking System, 2017 (http://vts.eocng.org).

legislators, and top officials into power through their control over the country's political grassroots. Governors can also play a spoiler role, undermining and toppling Abuja-based politicians who antagonize them. One of the main reasons President Jonathan's 2015 re-election bid failed was the defection of five governors from his party. Governors and ex-governors, many of whom grow very rich while in office, are also important party financiers. One such governor—now a minister—allegedly bankrolled President Buhari's 2015 presidential campaign.[3]

Governors' capacity for spreading patronage is rivaled only by the president. He (or she[4]) appoints a cabinet—usually consisting of at least one commissioner from each of the state's local government areas (LGAs)—as well as dozens of special advisers, special assistants, and senior civil servants known as permanent secretaries. Because of the size of their budgets and power to dole out lucrative state contracts, even seemingly humble state parastatals can become springboards to higher office. The longtime chairman of the Cross River State Water Board, for example, successfully parlayed his position into a senate seat in 2015. Likewise, the current governor of Abia

State was deputy director of the state environmental protection agency before running for office.

Historically, ruling party governors have also strongly influenced federal appointments—including ministerial positions and ambassadorships—though President Buhari appears to feel less bound by this convention than his predecessors. State governors also appoint state judges and name the salaried heads and board members of dozens of commissions, agencies, and parastatals. Following the death of any traditional chief or emir, the state governor must approve his replacement. As a result, some chieftaincy appointments have become politically charged, with some governors going so far as to create new titles or elevating existing ones in order to expand their patronage network.

Governors also exercise effective control over local government structures in their states, either by rigging local government elections or by finding excuses to postpone elections and appoint their cronies as interim "caretaker" chairmen instead. Most governors also enjoy free rein over local government finances through the "State Joint Local Government Account." Under the Nigerian constitution, local governments are supposed to receive nationally derived and some state-generated revenues through such accounts. In practice, however, state governors control these accounts, becoming their corrupt beneficiaries, rather than being trustees.[5] The result is that local government has become a moribund appendage of state government across most of Nigeria.

Governors are not all-powerful, however. They must deftly manage their relationships with the president and his coterie, as well as co-opt state legislators, civil servants, traditional leaders, local government chairmen, and security officials to hold on to power. Failure to do so can mean losing a re-election bid or even impeachment. One of the five governors who turned against Jonathan was impeached after disgruntled state legislators allegedly accepted bribes to unseat him. Similarly, four outgoing governors who mismanaged their political relationships failed to make the customary transition to the Senate during the 2015 election.

Unlike past presidents, President Buhari does not appear interested in using federal appointments and government contracts to build political patronage networks aimed at contesting governors' political influence in their states. He has also given a free hand to Nigeria's anticorruption agencies to investigate former governors and seize their ill-gotten gains. Even opposition party governors are tempering their criticism of the federal government, upon which they increasingly depend to bail out their recession-mired states.

Another arena in which federal officials and state governors should cooperate—yet where they sometimes compete—is security. Nigeria's myriad security challenges undermine state governance as much as they threaten national stability. Amid deteriorating security conditions—whether communal conflict in southern Kaduna State, banditry in Zamfara State, or rising crime in Cross River State—a governor must strike a delicate balance among negotiation, community engagement, and nudging the military and police to take action in a way that isn't counterproductive.

Unlike the federal government, state governors have no formal security powers and thus few tools with which to address insecurity beyond donating fuel, vehicles, and equipment to local police and military units that are otherwise neglected. Several governors have armed local civilians to serve as vigilantes, with mixed results. In Borno State, some observers credit these vigilantes with expelling Boko Haram from Maiduguri, even though human rights watchdogs claim they have committed extrajudicial killings and torture, citing gruesome videos and comments by vigilante leaders themselves.

Almost all governors pay for these ad hoc expenditures using multi-million-dollar "security votes": opaque slush funds that they have long used to embezzle state funds or redirect them for political purposes. Persistent insecurity therefore provides governors and their cronies with another mechanism for self-enrichment and spreading patronage.

Governors and their lieutenants, however, sometimes exacerbate local conflicts by sponsoring political thugs, showing ethnic bias, or neglecting simmering community disputes. This most notably occurred in Plateau State, the epicenter of communal conflict in Nigeria. During 2008 ethno-religious clashes in the state capital, Jos, then governor Jonah Jang ordered security forces to "shoot on sight."[6] Following his decree, soldiers and police allegedly carried out a wave of extrajudicial killings, increasing the death toll in the two-day crisis to over seven hundred.

How pervasive is official corruption?

Official corruption is more than conventional in Nigeria; it is endemic. It drains billions of dollars a year from the economy, stymies development, and weakens the social contract between the government and the people. Nigerians themselves view their country as one of the world's most corrupt, such that it perennially ranks in the bottom quartile of Transparency International's Corruption Perception Index. Reports and commentary about corruption are a staple of the country's vibrant news media as well as its literature, film, and music.

In Nigeria, official corruption takes many forms, from massive contract fraud to petty bribery, from straight-up embezzlement to complicated money laundering schemes, and from pocketing the salaries of fake ("ghost") workers to steering plum jobs to relatives and friends. Some officials enjoy perquisites so excessive that Nigerians widely see them as a form of legalized corruption. Others steal because they are obliged to pay off higher-ranking officials who could fire or reassign them if they fail to do so. In the words of one grizzled political veteran: "We control the operation of the money, that's all anybody's looking for. You may appropriate it rightly or wrongly. But there are certain things, even if they are wrong, they are conventional."[7]

Nor is official corruption a recent phenomenon. It is both a cause and a consequence of Nigeria's high-dollar politics, in which officeholders freely leverage their access to state funds to pad election war chests or recoup out-of-pocket campaign expenses.[8] It has thrived under both civilian and military-led governments and involves leaders of every ethnic and religious affiliation. Although corruption has saturated Nigeria's political culture, it isn't somehow organic to Nigerian culture. As anthropologist Daniel Jordan Smith argues, "Nigeria's is as much a culture *against* corruption as a culture *of* corruption" and is not "rooted in some sort of primordial traditional culture," nor is it viewed as "a desirable feature of everyday life."[9]

Although specific examples of official corruption abound, the following incident shows how glaring the scale of the theft can be and the facilitating role the international financial system plays. In 2005 British prosecutors charged former Bayelsa State governor D. S. P. Alamieyeseigha for using British shell companies and bank accounts to launder $3.4 million—a princely sum given his salary was just $32,000 a year. Police later found $1.9 million in cash stashed in a London penthouse he owned. Skipping bail, Alamieyeseigha absconded back to Nigeria, reportedly disguised as a woman. Though he was subsequently impeached and convicted in Nigeria on corruption charges, President Goodluck Jonathan pardoned Alamieyeseigha—his erstwhile political godfather—in 2013.

More often than not, corrupt officials like Alamieyeseigha need help from subordinates, lawyers, bankers, businessmen, and accountants to steal public funds. Their felonious activities are frequently enabled or shielded by global financial institutions, anemic international anticorruption policies, and pliant judges. Nigerian kleptocrats deftly use both Nigerian banks and the international financial system—especially anonymous shell corporations and offshore tax havens—to launder stolen public funds and stash them overseas, often in the form of high-end real estate in London, Dubai, New York, and California. Despite possessing robust discretionary powers, the United States and United Kingdom rarely deny visas to corrupt officials, scrutinize their unexplained wealth, or take action to seize their ill-gotten gains. Given the impunity Nigeria's kleptocrats enjoy, it is no surprise that official corruption is so pervasive.

How effective are efforts to combat corruption?

Prior to Nigeria's 1999 return to civilian rule, successive governments made little effort to combat corruption. One controversial exception was Muhammadu Buhari, who as military head of state (December 1983–August 1985) mounted a nationwide anticorruption campaign, arresting and imprisoning hundreds of officials from his predecessor, civilian president Shehu Shagari's, toppled government. Buhari's crusade was short-lived, however. Following his ouster, corruption blossomed under his successors, Generals Babangida (1985–1993) and Abacha (1993–1998).

Even though Babangida established the Code of Conduct Bureau (CCB)—Nigeria's first dedicated anticorruption body—it was not until President Obasanjo in 2000 established the Independent Corrupt Practices and Other Related Offences Commission (ICPC) and in 2003 the Economic and Financial Crimes Commission (EFCC) that a comprehensive approach to fighting official corruption began to take shape in Nigeria. The effectiveness of these institutions, however, oscillates with each management change and as political interference waxes and wanes.

Of these agencies, the EFCC plays the most prominent and effective role. Larger and better funded than its sister agencies, it enjoys a broad range of investigatory and law enforcement powers. Roughly twenty-two hundred strong, the EFCC is predominantly staffed by personnel on loan from the Nigeria Police Force (NPF).[10] While it has made headlines by arresting grasping politicians and errant bureaucrats, the commission also routinely investigates and prosecutes individuals involved in Internet scams, currency counterfeiting, and a wide range of other financial crimes. It works closely with and receives training from UK, US, and other international counterparts.

Though respected at home and abroad, the EFCC has nevertheless had its fair share of controversy. Even though it claims to have secured more than fifteen hundred convictions since 2003, the EFCC has at times struggled to convert its investigations and arrests into successful prosecutions.[11] Critics allege successive presidents have used the commission to go after their political rivals—or pressured it to turn a blind eye to their allies' misdeeds.[12] Indeed, diplomatic and civil society reports suggest one former chairperson was herself involved in facilitating corruption.[13] More recently, the EFCC has faced criticism for its opaque handling of billions of dollars in forfeited assets.

Although its remit awkwardly overlaps with that of its better-known sibling, the ICPC is tasked with investigating citizen complaints about public corruption—even at its most petty. Staffed by civil servants—vice policemen—the ICPC must work through the attorney general's office to prosecute cases, whereas the EFCC can do so independently. The ICPC also has two important, but often overlooked, secondary missions: partnering with civil society and the general public on anticorruption efforts and working with other government agencies to help them identify vulnerabilities and reduce corruption risks. It is these "soft power" capabilities that somewhat differentiate the ICPC from its more assertive counterpart, the EFCC.

The CCB, by contrast, gathers and attempts to validate asset declarations made by public officeholders at prescribed intervals during their careers. It is also tasked with ensuring that public officials abide by a fourteen-point code of conduct that prohibits them from having conflicts of interests; collecting more than one official salary; holding foreign bank accounts; or accepting gifts, private loans, or kickbacks. The CCB reports any breaches of this code to the attorney general for prosecution in the Code of Conduct Tribunal (CCT), an independent court.

The CCB's greatest flaw is that its work takes place in secret: officials' asset declarations are not subject to public scrutiny, including via Freedom of Information Act requests.[14] Even the crusading Buhari government has claimed, just like its predecessors, that the constitution—which authorizes the CCB to "make them available for inspection by any citizen of Nigeria"—prevents it from publishing asset declarations.[15] This leaves civil society organizations and private citizens with little choice other than to blindly trust the government to police itself.

In light of their overlapping and complementary roles, wouldn't it make sense to merge the EFCC, ICPC, and CCB into one well-resourced, full-spectrum anticorruption agency? The answer hinges on whether such a mega-agency would be endowed with the political independence, financial resources, and legal mandate needed to function more effectively than its forerunner organizations. Any new, combined anticorruption body would have to be carefully designed to ensure that the EFCC's investigation and prosecution mission does not overshadow the ICPC's prevention and public engagement functions or the CCB's oversight role.

Even if such institutional reforms take place, Nigerian efforts to combat corruption will still face a significant obstacle: a judiciary notorious for accepting bribes and awarding favorable rulings to the highest bidder. There are signs, however, that the executive arm of the government is working to rein in judicial corruption; in late 2016, the State Security Service arrested several senior judges after it discovered bags full of cash during raids on their homes.[16]

In addition to keeping bags full of cash, Nigerian kleptocrats often use the international financial system to funnel their ill-gotten gains abroad. Using opaque US shell corporations, anonymous holding companies domiciled in UK crown dependencies, or no-questions-asked cash deposits in Emirati banks, Nigerian elites are free to use their stolen assets to buy multi-million-dollar properties in London, luxury goods in New York, and high-end apartments in Dubai.

Since Nigeria-based corruption has such a significant foreign dimension, combating it will require developing a comprehensive set of international solutions. Despite its enthusiasm following President Buhari's 2015 election victory, however, the international community has yet to translate its fulsome praise of his much-vaunted anticorruption agenda into meaningful policy steps.

Instead of ratcheting up their anticorruption efforts, international partners' efforts remain broad based and untargeted, centered on modest assistance programs to investigators and civil society.[17] By not directly confronting corruption using travel bans and financial sanctions, the international community has done little to prevent kleptocrats from undermining Nigeria's political, security, and economic stability.

What distinguishes Nigeria's two dominant political parties?

The answer to this question is: surprisingly little. Nigeria's two main political parties—the ruling APC and the opposition PDP—share many of the same characteristics. Both are constellations of constantly shifting networks of national, state, and local elites. Both are almost identically structured, nonideological organizations made up of squabbling factions united in uneasy communion. Neither finances election campaigns transparently. Neither values internal party democracy, allowing money and high-level interference to corrupt candidate selection processes.

The APC and PDP also share much of the same DNA. With their supporters in tow, Nigerian politicians routinely cross the aisle from one party to the other—also known as "decamping" or "cross-carpeting"—in pursuit of new opportunities and financial resources. "In politics, there are no permanent friends and no permanent enemies" is a favorite saying among the nation's political class. An extreme example of this phenomenon is the Sokoto State politician who served as the state chairman of three different political parties in the space of four years. Politicians cross-carpeted with alacrity in the run-up to the 2015 elections, even doing so on the eve of party primaries in the case of the APC's governorship candidates in at least two states.

Since the early 1950s Nigerian political parties have either coalesced around a particular ethnogeographic base or emerged out of alliances between such groups. The one exception was during the short-lived Third Republic (1991–1993), when two national parties were artificially imposed by the Babangida regime. Strongly influenced by political veterans active since the 1970s, both parties can trace connections to these regionally anchored parties and still draw on political networks forged many decades ago.

In the brief run-up to Nigeria's 1999 return to civilian rule, the PDP united many of these old networks, winning the presidency and many governorships. Brimming with hundreds of wealthy, well-connected national and state politicians, the PDP went on to adeptly use petrodollar-fueled patronage, election rigging, and opposition infighting to stay in power for the next sixteen years. Like long-serving incumbent parties around the world, the PDP's popularity steadily declined—most notably after President Goodluck Jonathan attempted to eliminate popular fuel subsidies in 2012.

Over the next three years, accusations of grand corruption, the unchecked rise of Boko Haram, and widespread economic discontent eroded public support for Jonathan and the PDP. To make matters worse, Jonathan was mismanaging the once-dominant party's internal affairs, sowing discord, and alienating key PDP powerbrokers. After the party experienced massive defections in late 2013, Jonathan tried to re-energize the party with cash diverted from the petroleum and security sectors, but failed to avert a decisive poll defeat eighteen months later. Since losing the presidency, its Senate and House majority, and several governorships, the PDP has been beset by infighting and struggled to adapt to life as an opposition party. Former president Obasanjo even went as far to declare the party "dead, sunk, and gone."[18]

Down though it may be, the PDP is almost certainly not out. The party's somewhat derelict apparatus could be reinvigorated if it can re-establish a viable nationwide political coalition. It has a firm grip on sources of party funds: several state governorships, the position of deputy senate president, and dozens of lucrative Senate and House committee chairmanships. Support for the PDP remains unwavering across much of the Niger Delta region and the ethnically Igbo southeast. Although northern support for the PDP has eroded in recent years, it remains more robust than the support the APC enjoys in the PDP's southern strongholds.

The ruling APC, in contrast, is a younger but equally unstable political construct. It was established in July 2013 when three regionally rooted parties—the southwest-oriented Action Congress of Nigeria (ACN) as well as the northern-focused All Nigeria Peoples Party (ANPP) and Congress for Progressive Change (CPC)—united under its banner.[19] In November 2013 five PDP governors—including those in charge of the vote-rich Kano and wealthy Rivers states—along with former vice president Atiku Abubakar and dozens of legislators, defected to the APC, greatly boosting its political strength in the run-up to the 2015 election. The APC won the 2015 election on a broadly populist platform, promising a wide range of public sector–driven solutions to the country's greatest economic, infrastructure, and social challenges. It also tapped into widespread public anger over extreme levels of government corruption.

In addition to its two mega-parties, Nigeria has many smaller ones. Some of these parties have a specific regional base. Many subsist from one election to the next by renting themselves out as "vehicles" so PDP or APC primary losers can have a second chance to contest national or state elections.

Others are used by ambitious politicians to build support in the hope that they will become enough of a spoiler to be co-opted by one of the major parties. Nevertheless, in some states third parties are genuinely competitive. The All Progressives Grand Alliance (APGA) has governed Anambra State since 2006. In Adamawa State, the People's Democratic Movement (PDM) made a strong showing in the 2015 governorship elections, coming in second ahead of the PDP. The Accord Party, meanwhile, once enjoyed significant support in Oyo State.

As the 2019 elections approach, some presidential hopefuls may establish new parties—or breathe new life into dormant ones—and try to attract high-profile defectors from the APC, the PDP, or both. Because Nigerian law prohibits independent (nonparty) candidates, established parties will remain preeminent, acting as middlemen in the democratic process. Likewise, by allowing thuggery and "cash-and-carry politics" to erode internal party democracy, party leaders limit voter choice and perpetuate a venal political class, thereby hurting Nigeria's overall democratic development.

Are Nigerian elections free and fair?

Since the restoration of civilian governance in 1999, Nigeria has held presidential elections every four years and numerous ad hoc state and local polls in between. The constitution requires that to be elected president, a candidate has to win the most votes but also must win 25 percent of the votes in two-thirds of the states. This requirement was designed to require a successful candidate to appeal beyond his or her own ethnic and religious constituency. If no candidate meets these two requirements, there is a provision in the constitution for a run-off vote; however, that has not happened in Nigeria's short democratic history.

Massive election rigging by rival elites has been characteristic of Nigeria since independence. Indeed, rigging has been an important element of elite competition. The intraparty candidate selection process, election day, and ballot counting have all often been the occasion for extensive violence. Rivals for a party's nomination have been murdered. Voter registration lists have been inflated, ballot boxes stuffed, and the integrity of collation centers regularly compromised. Even during the 2015 elections, generally regarded as the best since the restoration of civilian government, there was widespread rigging, especially in the Niger Delta region and parts of the southeast.

In a country with a deteriorating national infrastructure and a rapidly growing population, elections are a major logistical challenge. The constitution charges the Independent National Electoral Commission (INEC) with the conduct of elections. By 2015 INEC had a full-time staff of 14,000, making it one of the country's largest government agencies. In addition, INEC recruits an additional 300,000 people for ad hoc election duty. In the elections of 1999, 2003, 2007, and 2011, the incumbent president exercised considerable influence over INEC. However, INEC under the chairmanship of Prof. Attahiru Jega and with international assistance is credited with delivering credible 2015 national elections in which, for the first time, an opposition candidate was elected president. A respected elections expert, Jega introduced significant technical and procedural changes that improved the voting and counting process, greatly reducing—though not eliminating—opportunities for rigging. In the aftermath of the 2015 elections, INEC enjoyed widespread popularity even beyond the elites.

With late colonial roots, INEC has been regularly modified and reformed, ostensibly to increase its independence and its efficiency. Such initiatives were largely ones of form rather than substance. However, Nigeria's elite political culture has been evolving toward credible elections, not least because of the legitimacy they confer on an administration. Accordingly, INEC is now funded directly from the Federation Account, giving it substantial financial independence. However, the president still appoints its chairman and the twelve national commissioners. Governors, in turn, appoint state electoral commissioners who run local elections. Its critics maintain that because of presidential and gubernatorial appointment authority, INEC does not yet enjoy complete independence from the executive. However, there is an elite conversation nationwide about how to ensure greater independence for INEC in the future.

In a society organized around patronage/clientage networks, few voters have been genuinely free to vote their preferences. Instead, they have followed the lead of their patrons. On occasion elite and popular enthusiasm coincides. In 2015 the elites reached a consensus in much of the country that President Jonathan had to go, and they organized the votes of their dependents accordingly. At the same time, there was genuine popular enthusiasm "on the street" for Buhari, especially in the north.

Before 2015 it could hardly be said that Nigerian elections were free and fair. Many people stayed away from the polls. Usually about half of the eligible electorate or fewer voters cast their ballots. In 2015 the voting process was firmly under elite control, and there was much less competitive rigging. There was a much larger popular dimension and enthusiasm about the process because of Buhari's personal popularity across large parts of the country and his reputation for incorruptibility.

What is a day in the life of a Nigerian politician like?

Though long, exhausting, and thankless, a day in the life of a Nigerian politician is also replete with opportunities for self-aggrandizement and self-enrichment. If politicians want to stay relevant and have a chance at re-election, they must adeptly juggle the demands of their day jobs with round-the-clock politicking in the form of courtesy visits, incessant phone calls and text messages, and late-night strategy sessions.

Unless politicians deliver a steady stream of public goods (i.e., roads, schools, power and water projects) and private patronage in the form of money for school fees, wedding gifts, medical bills, and foodstuffs ("stomach infrastructure"), their constituents will grumble that they are not "performing" and not "generous." At the same time, federal and state legislators complain that their constituents' expectations are unreasonable, that they do not have unlimited financial resources and have few opportunities to steer government projects back home.

For new entrants, running for office requires waging a grassroots campaign to win over local power brokers and opinion makers who will help get out the vote—or suppress the other candidates' vote—on election day. Here's how one commentator described a candidate's first foray ("entry behavior") into local politics:

> Begin frequent visits home. Stock up on bags of rice and salt, posh mobile phones, recharge cards. Stock up on expensive alcoholic drinks. Sink a borehole [well] or two. Start attending funerals, chieftaincy parties, church/ mosque dedications. Pay some school fees—but only at the primary and secondary school levels. . . . After about a year of this, step up the frequency of your visits home . . . take your expensive drinks and your [bags full of cash] and begin to visit the stakeholders . . . the ward [party] chairmen, ward [party] secretaries, women leaders and youth leaders and do the needful.[20]

Financing this kind of retail politicking is expensive, making any run for office—even at the local level—a risky financial undertaking. First-time candidates must take out loans; sell assets; or ask friends, relatives, and business contacts to help fund their campaigns and pay the exorbitant fees that national, state, and local party officials charge candidates seeking nomination forms to run. One national party official described the almost parasitic role party officials play as follows:

> People who want to run for office . . . virtually bankroll the parties in their localities. Sometimes they even decide who becomes the chairman in their ward. . . . They

actually pocket the person, they take care of his daily needs. Those are the informal ways that party officials run their lives because mostly they have no other business other than running the party . . . through this very indecent manner.[21]

In order for their candidacy to be taken seriously, politicians must spread money and gifts among local powerbrokers, party officials, delegates who vote in party primaries, community groups, and even voters themselves. Opposition party candidates face especially long odds. "When you run as an opposition person, it's very difficult because those in government use state funds. You can't compete with them," lamented one candidate who spent 7 million naira ($40,000 in 2014) running for a state house of assembly seat in 2015 and lost.[22]

A big chunk of any Nigerian politician's day is spent cultivating and maintaining relationships with powerbrokers higher up the political food chain. These include top-tier political financiers, usually ministers or other presidential appointees who occupy lucrative ("juicy") jobs from which they can easily divert state funds. They may even include presidents past and present—vice presidents, the First Lady, ministers, and national party leaders who have the power to sway party primary—or even general election—outcomes. Politicians must also cultivate friendships with key individuals in the election commission, security forces, and judiciary who could help influence the outcome of a closely contested election. One former governor described how a hypothetical first-term governor might seek to co-opt the top election official in his state for this purpose as follows:

When the Resident Electoral Commissioner (REC) comes before the elections are conducted . . . he pays a courtesy call on the governor. It's usually a televised event you know, and of course he says all the right things: "Your Excellency, I am here to ensure that we have free and fair elections and I will require your support." After the courtesy call, the REC now moves in for a one-on-one with the governor the says, "Your Excellency, since I came, I've been staying in this hotel, there is no accommodation for me and even my vehicle is broken down and the last Commissioner didn't leave the vehicle. . . ." The Governor says [to his Chief of Staff]: "Please ensure that the REC is accommodated. Put him in the Presidential lodge, allot two cars to him. . . ." A few weeks to the elections, the REC sees the governor . . . and says, "we need to conduct a training programme for the [polling unit] presiding officers and headquarters hasn't sent us any money yet, you know. . . ." [The governor asks:] "How much would that cost?" The REC replies: "N25 million [$170,000 as of 2010] for the first batch, we may have about three batches." [Calling his Chief of Staff, the governor says:] "Make sure that we arrange N25 million this week . . . and N75 million in all . . . put it under 'Security Vote'." In other words . . . cash in huge Ghana Must Go bags.[23]

Once elected, politicians face enormous pressure to reward their supporters and kin, assuage former opponents ("carry people along"), and infuse money into their political support apparatus ("structure"). This structure typically includes state and local party entities, community groups such as market vendors (many of whom are women) and transport workers, local youth, and sympathetic religious and traditional leaders. Politicians often build personal support organizations that operate parallel to—but outside—political party structures in case they someday need to switch parties ("decamp" or "cross-carpet") to realize their ambitions. These kinds of political structures are almost entirely fueled by politicians' sustained financial patronage. Without it, they risk being seen as not "on ground" as the loyalty, enthusiasm, and political usefulness of their neglected structures fade.

Some politicians, in contrast, have very little structure, relying on powerful patrons ("godfathers") to help realize their ambitions. In the run-up to an election, godfathers can be a huge political asset, providing candidates with financial and political muscle they could not otherwise muster. State governors often play this godfather role, attempting to name ("anoint") their successors or tapping their loyalists as legislative candidates ("giving them a ticket"). After the election, however, these relationships frequently sour as the godfathers' political interests—and those of their newly empowered godchildren—diverge, splitting state and local party structures into factions. This can leave godfather-less politicians scrambling to forge new alliances and rebuild their political support structures from scratch.

It is no surprise that Nigerian officeholders, distracted by political intrigues, focus little on actual governing and policymaking during an average day. Even when they do, political considerations often loom large. No politician wants to be labeled "an Abuja politician" who "cannot win his own polling unit," which is code for someone who risks election defeat because he has ignored his constituents. Nor can politicians afford to be complacent as they climb the "greasy pole" of Nigerian politics, lest a more cunning opponent send them sliding back down.

Other than through the ballot box, how can Nigerians influence politics?

There is a distinction to be made between elite and popular politics. Elites direct or influence politics through patronage networks, access to oil revenue, and control of much—but not all—of the media. They also dominate the political parties, the National Assembly, and the judiciary. Much of the modern economy is in their hands. High-ranking military officers are usually part of these elite networks. Hence elites have many ways to influence a presidential administration. However, as is Nigerian society in general, elites are usually divided among themselves. It is rare that they unify over a specific political issue. It does happen, however, such as when they were relatively united over preventing President Obasanjo's 2006 effort to secure a third term.

Nigerians outside the elites have only limited influence over politics. Some are active in the country's many civil society organizations (CSOs) and NGOs. During the years of military rule, civilian entities like the Transition Monitoring Group helped facilitate a return to democracy, and the Nigerian Bar Association doubled as the country's largest human rights organization. Other professional and academic organizations and religious umbrella groups, both Christian and Muslim, can be influential on specific issues. Nigeria's CSOs tend to be much stronger and more influential in the southern, predominantly Christian half of the country than in the north. In part, civil society strength reflects the more developed economy and higher levels of formal education in the south. However, elites themselves often come to dominate civil organizations. Highly paid professionals dominate legal, medical, and academic organizations and themselves are a part of elite networks.

The trade unions, through strikes, can force the government to reverse or modify its policies. They, too, are strongest in the south, especially in the oil patch, where their capacity to shut down oil production guarantees government attention. However, successive governments have effectively managed the trade unions through a carrot-and-stick strategy of payoffs and repression.

Nigeria's media are free, vibrant, and uncensored. For most Nigerians, radio is the most important news source. In addition to government-owned networks, there are numerous private stations. Television is mostly government owned and is largely an elite medium featuring sports and, often, American reruns. Al-Jazeera, BBC, Deutsche Welle, Radio France International, and the Voice of America broadcast freely. Even in remote parts of the country, many Nigerians are well informed about world events. However, violence against media personnel is common and goes largely unpunished, reflecting the weak law enforcement capacity of the state. Newspapers are expensive, but each copy is passed from hand to hand and has many readers. Many print media are owned by the politically connected, and news is often for sale to the highest bidder. The "brown envelope scheme" refers to the common practice of buying favorable media coverage in which politicians hand journalists cash in brown envelopes. Building journalistic integrity remains a work in progress.

Specific issues can overcome the usual myriad divisions among Nigerians. For example, President Jonathan's attempt in January 2012 to reduce the government's subsidy on the price of gas and kerosene united nonelite Nigerians across religious and ethnic divisions and forced a partial rollback. During demonstrations against ending the fuel subsidy, there were incidents of Christians protecting Muslims at prayer time. Civil society anger over the Jonathan administration's seeming inaction in response to Boko Haram's kidnapping of more than two hundred schoolgirls led to daily demonstrations and the launch of a social media based movement ("#BringBackOurGirls"). Traditional rulers, with little formal power, can be highly influential in specific geographic areas because of the respect they continue to receive from their subjects.

Are women a force in Nigerian politics?

Even though they are a powerful grassroots political constituency, women could be much more of a force in Nigerian politics than they are now. Currently, women are woefully underrepresented across Nigeria's three tiers of government. Defying simple explanation, this marginalization is the complex product of the country's money politics, its legacy of military rule, and its patriarchal social structures, especially in the north.

Given the powerful role money, patronage, and old boys' networks play in fueling Nigerian political careers, the pre-eminence of men has been somewhat self-perpetuating. Beyond the office of the first lady—whose influence grew exponentially under Mrs. Babangida and Mrs. Abacha—women occupied only a handful of official positions up until the country's 1999 return to civilian rule. Unlike legions of male former military officials and civilian officeholders, most female political aspirants lack the wealth needed to be successful in election campaigns. At the grassroots level very few working women have had the economic freedom and financial means needed to "catapult" them into formal political roles.[24]

In addition to the wealth gap, women seeking to enter public life face another significant obstacle: run-of-the-mill gender bias. Even the First Lady was recently chided by her husband for talking politics when he said "I don't know which party my wife belongs to, but she belongs to my kitchen, and my living room, and the other room." The president's comments went viral and "the other room" has since entered the Nigerian popular lexicon. At the political grassroots, this kind of attitude often stems from traditional ideas about gender roles. In the words of a woman legislator from rural central Nigeria:

> In my local constituency, you have these meetings every morning where men come together . . . in the early morning and when they discuss and have a drink and before they go on their business. Women are not part of such meetings. So [men] would always use that as an instance, "How would a wom[a]n be in that meeting? This is not a meeting for women." And so the struggle is to say "Oh no, women can do this, and women can also represent you at this level. They have equal brains, they can talk, all that you need for somebody that can say your problems."[25]

In the eighteen years since the country's return to civilian rule, no state has elected a female governor. In 2007 Nigerians set a dismal—but as yet unbroken—record when they elected 9 women to the 109-member Senate. By 2015, however, that number had fallen to a mere 6. Women hold a similarly small fraction of seats in the federal House of Representatives and thirty-six state legislatures. Nigeria is among a handful of countries with the lowest proportion of female legislators worldwide. Women occupy a smaller share of seats than in Iran—an ultraconservative theocracy—not to mention North Korea, Somalia, and Syria.[26]

Those remarkable women who have successfully climbed to the top of the greasy pole of Nigerian politics have taken different paths to get there. Several have leveraged their family names and political structures. Some have parlayed international accomplishments into political careers. A few have even defied the odds by patiently but doggedly working their way from the bottom up. The following are a few of their stories.

Scions. Gbemisola Saraki hails from a powerful political family in Kwara State. Her father, Olusola Saraki, was the prototypical Nigerian political godfather and wheeler-dealer. Gbemisola's brother Bukola Saraki was governor for eight years (2003–2011) and is now Senate president. Elected to the House in 1999 and the Senate in 2003, Gbemisola leveraged her father's and brother's extensive political networks and deep pockets. In 2011 her political career ran aground, not solely because of her gender, but rather because of her brother's desire to appropriate her Senate seat for himself and install one of his protégés as governor instead of her. Although Gbemisola has since reconciled with her brother, her experiences show that even those women from Nigeria's most powerful political dynasties are not immune from its rough-and-tumble politics.

Outsiders. Though descended from Yoruba royalty, Monsurat Sunmonu emigrated to the United Kingdom as a young woman, whereupon she embarked on a successful career working for the Home Office. In 2011 she returned home, successfully campaigning for a seat in the Oyo State legislature. For the next four years as the assembly's first female speaker, Sunmonu used her international management experience to lead the fractious body, which was almost evenly split among three rival parties. In 2015 she was one of just seven women to win election to the Senate, where she became the chair of its foreign affairs committee.

Gladiators. Margaret Ekpo is one of Nigeria's pioneer female politicians. An activist at heart, Ekpo helped unionize market women and mobilize women's groups across southeastern Nigeria, encouraging them to take a more active role in colonial politics.[27] After independence, Ekpo competed against seven men to win a regional assembly seat in 1962. As she has described the situation:

> Campaigning around the country as a woman was not easy. Sometimes, our opponents would send thugs to throw stones, bottles and sticks at us. . . . It was not at all easy, but we had to do it . . . so that women could begin to enjoy some of their entitlements today. . . . [As a legislator] I tabled many motions, argued, and got some of them passed into laws. My accomplishments paved the way for women who were interested in pursuing political careers, and motivated them to do so with greater confidence.[28]

Fifty years later, political leaders are acutely aware of Nigerian women's grassroots mobilizing power. Often using their wives as proxies, top politicians seeking to energize this power voting bloc court market women's associations, military and police wives' clubs, and faith-based groups in the run-up to elections. During the 2015 election campaign, for example, First Lady Patience Jonathan claimed her husband's PDP was "the only party that has the interests of women at heart" and promised that her husband would give 45 percent "affirmative action" to women if re-elected.[29] Absent a quota system like this, however, the role of Nigerian women likely will remain peripheral until elections become more fair and credible, political parties become more open, and popularity supplants money as a candidate's most important asset.

5

NIGERIA'S SECURITY CHALLENGES

Some of Nigeria's greatest security threats—such as Boko Haram and militancy in the oil-rich Niger Delta—routinely grab international headlines. Others, like deadly communal conflict and violent crime, rarely do. Nevertheless, these security challenges have something in common: all are a product of Nigerian state weakness, especially corruption, poor governance, widespread policing failures, and elite sponsorship of violence entrepreneurs.

What are Nigeria's top security challenges?

Nigeria's most serious and widespread security challenge is perhaps its least well understood: communal violence. This term is most often used to describe land disputes involving farmers and herdsmen or between rival ethnic communities. The proliferation of small arms and the mobilization of youth gangs associated with communal violence frequently beget a range of other security problems, such as political thuggery, armed robbery, cattle rustling, and kidnapping for ransom.

In northeastern Nigeria, violence perpetrated by the terrorist group Boko Haram continues to claim lives and immiserate more than two million displaced people. Soldiers and security operatives are deployed in harm's way, operating in difficult terrain amid vulnerable civilian populations. Even though the Nigerian Army (NA) is heavily deployed all across Borno State, Boko Haram somehow continues to terrorize rural villages, ambush military patrols, and conduct suicide bombings. Fears linger that Boko Haram could shift the focus of its attacks toward government or international targets in Abuja or toward N'djamena, the capital of Chad, located only about sixty miles over Nigeria's northeast border.

Though less deadly, a long-running insurgency by criminalized militants in the Niger Delta threatens the uninterrupted flow of the country's economic lifeblood: petroleum. Local communities are often caught in the crossfire between gun-toting militants and security personnel, even as they struggle with the effects of poverty, misgovernance, and environmental degradation caused by oil spills and gas flaring. Armed youths moonlight as oil thieves, sea pirates, and political thugs.

Under-resourced, sapped by corruption, distrusted by the population, and frequently heavy-handed, Nigeria's security forces are unable to safeguard a country more than twice the size of California. Nigeria's difficult geography—whether densely populated megacities like Lagos and Port Harcourt, labyrinthine mangrove swamps, mountainous hinterlands, or dense bushlands—offers safe haven to criminals, militants, and even terrorists.

Governance failures and official corruption—especially at the state level—also fuel insecurity across Nigeria by aggravating local grievances, eroding state legitimacy, and impoverishing communities, leaving them vulnerable to the predations of violent entrepreneurs like Boko Haram, Niger Delta militants, and other armed gangs.

What is Boko Haram, and why has it become so deadly?

Boko Haram is a jihadi terrorist group that has waged a deadly insurgency centered on the Lake Chad Basin since early 2010. The name "Boko Haram" is not one the group uses itself but rather a colloquialism meaning "Western education is forbidden by Islam."[1] The group instead called itself Jamā'at Ahl al-Sunnah li Da'wah wa-l-Jihād until 2015, when its leader aligned the group with the Islamic State in Syria (ISIS). Boko Haram's terror campaign has killed at least thirty thousand people since May 2011; thousands more Nigerian civilians have died as a result of government counterterrorism operations.[2]

Unlike other terrorist groups worldwide, we know very little about Boko Haram's structure, its internal workings, or the identities and mindset of its followers. The group rarely communicates with outsiders and has yielded few defectors. Much of what we do know about Boko Haram has been extrapolated from its activity patterns or derived from its ultra-Salafi founder Mohammed Yusuf's teachings, unverified media reporting and military statements, and its infamous propaganda videos.

Analysis of these clues tells us that Boko Haram's worldview is exclusivist: it thinks that Muslims should choose between their faith and secular practices it deems anti-Islamic, such as democracy, Western-style education, and interfaith cooperation.[3] Citing radical Salafi teachings, Boko Haram has also sought to justify its use of violence to pursue the overthrow of Nigeria's secular government.[4] Although its destructive—almost nihilist—agenda continues to evolve, the group's ideology is rooted in Yusuf's extreme beliefs.

Yusuf was a charismatic, self-educated preacher who fell out with his mentor, a mainstream Salafi cleric, over Yusuf's hard-line rejection of Western education and government employment.[5] A breakaway group of his followers—nicknamed the "Nigerian Taliban"—even attacked a rural police station in 2003, sparking swift military retaliation. Cassette recordings of Yusuf's fiery sermons condemning traditional Islamic authorities and government efforts to implement sharia law broadcast his extreme ideas well beyond his mosque in the Borno State capital, Maiduguri.

Over the next several years Yusuf's influence continued to grow. Then-governor Ali Modu Sheriff cultivated ties with Yusuf and his followers, appointing one of them to his cabinet.[6] This uneasy alliance began to unravel in 2007, however, culminating in a watershed moment in Boko Haram's development as a terrorist group: the July 2009 military crackdown that resulted in more than eight hundred deaths and the summary execution—videorecorded and posted on YouTube—of Mohammed Yusuf by police.[7]

Following the group's near extinction, Yusuf's remaining followers dispersed across the region or went into hiding in Maiduguri's poorest neighborhoods. Thirsty for revenge, these survivors attacked military and police patrols, enlisted new recruits, terrorized civilians, and assassinated political and religious figures. The group's new leaders began reaching out to Al-Qaeda in the Islamic Maghreb (AQIM) for training, funding, and operational expertise. This outreach was evident in the 2011 suicide bomb attack against a UN office building in Abuja, which killed twenty-one people.

In the wake of the UN bombing, the Nigerian government intensified its counterinsurgency operations in the northeast under the auspices of the military-led Joint Task Force Restore Order (JTF-RO), which in 2013 became a new army division. As Boko Haram attacks continued to escalate, Nigerian counterterrorism operations became more repressive. JTF-RO soldiers began rounding up young men and boys and deposited them in ad hoc prisons like Giwa Barracks in Maiduguri, where several thousand detainees died from starvation, disease, and torture in less than three years. Security force abuses did little to degrade the group, but rather succeeded in fueling its antigovernment narratives, bolstering its recruitment, and alienating Western allies.

It was in this context that Boko Haram made world headlines when it kidnapped more than two hundred female students from a secondary school in the town of Chibok in southern Borno State in April 2014. (See figure 5.1.) These tactics echoed those of a notorious slave raider—Hamman Yaji—who had terrorized the region as recently as the late 1920s, kidnapping and enslaving young girls in the name of Islam.[8] The plight of the Chibok schoolgirls quickly went viral on social media as celebrities, top politicians, and fellow schoolchildren worldwide urged the Nigerian government to "#BringBackOurGirls." In the months that followed, however, Boko Haram scored a series of victories against

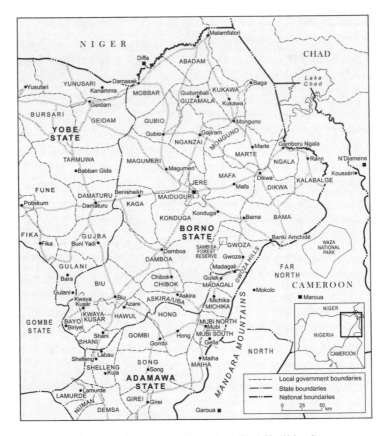

Figure 5.1 Key towns and villages in Borno State. (Credit: Cambridge University Cartographic Unit)

demoralized troops, whose capabilities had been eroded by years of corruption.

Seizing upon the weakness of the Nigerian state and its security apparatus, Boko Haram solidified its control over large parts of Borno, Yobe, and Adamawa states, pillaging and displacing or killing thousands as it went. Reacting to these developments, neighbors Chad and Niger in March 2015 launched a cross-border offensive that helped the Nigerian military regain lost territory and forced Boko Haram back into remote safe havens in rural Borno State, on the islands of Lake Chad, and in the Mandara Mountains of Cameroon. Weakened and on the run, Boko Haram's remaining fighters nevertheless continue to ambush military patrols and launch suicide bombings against civilian targets across the Lake Chad region. The group currently appears to be split into two factions that could be considered separate groups: one led by Yusuf's son Abu Musab Al-Barnawi, which sees itself as a branch of ISIS, and another led by Abubakar Shekau, which sees itself as more autonomous.

As this abbreviated account of the evolution of Boko Haram shows, the group became stronger and increasingly deadly as its ideology became more extreme, it exposed the weaknesses of the Nigerian state, and security force abuses alienated local populations. Boko Haram's Sisyphean insurgency has been doubly deadly, insofar as the Nigerian government's counterinsurgency missteps and heavy-handed tactics have brought death and destruction to many of the same communities it was supposed to protect.

Even more deadly than the struggle between Boko Haram and the Nigerian military, however, is the far-reaching humanitarian crisis it has precipitated. As of 2017, the conflict has displaced roughly two million people in northeastern Nigeria; rendered millions more at risk of famine; and destabilized parts of eastern Niger, Chad, and northern Cameroon.[9] The crisis has particularly affected women, who already enjoyed few economic and educational opportunities and experienced the world's highest infant and maternal mortality rates. Mismanagement, corruption, and infighting between the Nigerian government and international relief organizations have exacerbated the crisis, even as huge numbers of young children have died of starvation.[10] Until these problems are solved and the humanitarian crisis abates, the Boko Haram conflict will remain one of the world's deadliest, even if the group itself has been relegated to the shadows, albeit with the capacity to regroup and resurge as it has in the past.

What are the roots of the Niger Delta militancy?

Niger Delta militancy evolved as the result of a toxic mix of deep grievances over the exploitation of the Niger Delta region, endemic governance failures, and criminality. Despite living amid the source of Nigeria's great oil wealth, the people of the Niger Delta remain deeply impoverished, struggling to cope with pollution caused by gas flaring and oil spills. Decades of poor governance and unbridled political corruption have fueled criminality, sparked communal conflict, and compounded the region's socioeconomic challenges. For years, militant and criminal activity has been incentivized by elites, either by direct sponsorship or through conciliatory payoffs. Nonviolent actors have been marginalized. Together, these factors have fueled Niger Delta militancy, immiserating local people and threatening the oil production that is the lifeblood of Nigeria's finances.

It is difficult to pinpoint when the region's troubles started. Conflict between ethnic groups—particularly the Ijaw and Itsekiri people—dates back centuries, to the time when European traders privileged the Itsekiri as middlemen in the slave and palm oil trade. In the western Niger Delta, British colonial authorities further marginalized the Ijaw by elevating Itsekiri chiefs to rule over them.[11] And while a colonial fact-finding commission noted that the region's unique challenges were "poorly understood" by faraway officials, it stopped short of recommending "political arrangements that would unite in one political unit the whole body of Ijaws."[12]

The start of commercial oil production in 1958—and independence from British colonial rule two years later—sharpened calls from the Niger Delta for greater political representation and resource control. In 1966 a young policeman named Isaac Adaka Boro declared a "Niger Delta Republic," leading a quixotic rebellion that was quashed after just twelve days. Revered by many Ijaw today, Boro believed that the region's inhabitants deserved to benefit from its enormous oil wealth.

Three decades later, writer turned activist Ken Saro-Wiwa spearheaded a movement protesting the environmental and socioeconomic problems caused by Royal Dutch Shell's operations in his Ogoni people's home area. In 1995 Sani Abacha—Nigeria's corrupt and repressive head of state—had Saro-Wiwa and eight colleagues ("The Ogoni Nine") convicted by a kangaroo court and executed.[13] Their deaths sparked an international outcry and fueled popular discontent across the Niger Delta, setting the stage for the 1998 Kaiama Declaration, a catalog of grievances and demands announced by Ijaw activists. One year later, a military crackdown against the troublemaking town of Odi left hundreds of civilians dead, deepening these grievances.

Over the next decade, militancy flourished as politicians armed and employed militants to rig elections and threaten opponents. Two of the region's oldest militant groups—Ateke Tom's Niger Delta Vigilante and the Dokubo Asari's Niger Delta People's Volunteer Force—played this role during the 2003 Rivers State elections. When not stealing ballots and intimidating voters, these and other militant outfits kidnapped foreign oil workers and local bigwigs for ransom, operated protection rackets, and facilitated oil theft. During this period, militants developed symbiotic relationships with rival criminal gangs ("cults"), ugly mutations of decades-old university fraternities whose colorful names—Icelandos, Greenlanders, Deebam, Deewell—belie their appetite for extreme violence.

In December 2005 a new umbrella militant group—the Movement for the Emancipation of the Niger Delta (MEND)—debuted, making international headlines by blowing up key oil installations and conducting high-profile kidnappings. Publicity-savvy from the start, MEND's public profile continued to rise, fueled by press releases from "Jomo Gbomo," the group's faceless spokesperson, who vowed to "totally destroy the capacity of the Nigerian government to export oil."[14] Over the next three years periodic MEND attacks disrupted Nigerian oil production, sending already high global crude oil prices even higher. State politicians' covert links to militant groups expanded, and popular discontent over resource control, poverty, and environmental degradation continued to grow even after Goodluck Jonathan, an ethnic Ijaw from Bayelsa State, became vice president in 2007.

In May 2009 the Nigerian government changed its Niger Delta strategy when it launched a major military strike against Camp Five, a key MEND operational base overseen by businessman turned warlord Tompolo. This decision could have escalated the conflict; military crackdowns typically exacerbate local grievances and result in civilian deaths and property destruction rather than yielding long-term security gains. By signaling its intent to escalate the conflict militarily—while at the same time offering to absolve militants willing to lay down their arms—the Nigerian government, in October 2009, successfully concluded an amnesty with all but a few of the region's militants.

Almost a decade on, it is unclear if this surprisingly durable—albeit mismanaged and corruption-prone—program has succeeded in disarming, demobilizing, and rehabilitating the region's most violence-prone youth. Despite their effectiveness, tools like the amnesty and pipeline security contracts given to former militants inadvertently incentivize attacks by up-and-coming groups seeking to become enough of a threat to be given a stipend, a contract, or even a seat at the negotiating table. By threatening the country's oil output, even the most ambitious of upstart militant groups might find themselves eligible for government payoffs and patronage. The region's first-generation militant leaders, meanwhile, are seeking to clean up their public image, with some even launching political careers. In Delta State, for example, Kingsley Otuaro, a former top lieutenant of MEND mastermind Tompolo, became deputy governor. In Rivers State, former militant leader Farah Dagogo is now a state legislator.

This could explain why, following President Buhari's 2015 election win, unrest in the Niger Delta resumed. The violence slashed already declining production as previously unknown militant groups like the Niger Delta Avengers attacked oil infrastructure using relatively sophisticated tactics. In July 2016, for example, militants used diving gear to sabotage a key pipeline at a major crude oil export terminal that was one hundred meters underwater—an unprecedented feat. Even though these new groups have ties to former MEND figures and have co-opted historical symbols like Isaac Adaka Boro, they have struggled to build a truly regional militant movement, constrained by the region's sharp ethnic divides.

Looking ahead, it is clear that no combination of "carrots and sticks" (e.g., security crackdowns and government payouts) is capable of addressing the complex roots of Niger Delta militancy, which span a range of socioeconomic grievances, criminal motivations, and governance failures. Instead, Nigeria's three tiers of government, the petroleum industry, and Niger Delta communities themselves must collaborate to decrease tensions, sideline violent actors, and address issues of common concern—like mitigating environmental damage—while continuing to negotiate about more contentious ones, like sharing oil revenues.

Why has communal conflict killed so many Nigerians?

Communal conflict has become one of Nigeria's most deadly and destabilizing security challenges because its causes are so varied, complex, and localized. Although no part of Nigeria is immune from these disputes and outbreaks of violence, areas located along ethnic fault lines like the Middle Belt are especially vulnerable. According to one study, sixty-five separate incidents of communal violence occurred in Nigeria in 2016 alone.[15] Heightened competition over political representation and access to resources—whether land, petroleum revenues, or market space—has also fueled intercommunal conflict. Instead of intervening constructively to help resolve local disputes before they boil over, security personnel and government officials often either fail to act or take steps that aggravate tensions.

The origins of communal conflict fall into three broad categories: land disputes, battles over resources (oil, water, market space), and political disagreements. Although these clashes are often framed in ethno-religious terms, their root causes invariably can be distilled down to one or more of these three.

Land disputes. Whether a product of population growth, climate change, or internal displacement, day-to-day struggles over land access, use, and ownership are common all across Nigeria. Such disputes between farmers and seminomadic livestock herders are centuries old but have recently flared as competition for land and water grows. Spurred on by Nigerians' ever-increasing demand for beef and dairy, cattle grazers and their sizeable herds are ranging farther south than ever before, upsetting farming communities in their path. For their part, farmers facing similar economic and environmental pressures have antagonized herdsmen by planting crops on established grazing reserves or astride ancient cattle routes. Land feuds do not just involve herdsmen, however; they even spark deadly violence between neighboring farming communities that share close ethnic ties: Umuleri and Aguleri in Anambra State and Ezza and Ezillo in Ebonyi State, for example.[16]

Resource battles. Land is not the only resource that sparks conflict between communities. In the oil-rich Niger Delta, neighboring communities frequently clash over access to oil infrastructure and the employment, support contracts, oil company largesse—and even oil theft opportunities—that come with it. In western Delta State, smoldering territorial disputes between the neighboring Ijaw and Itsekiri ethnic groups center on areas dotted with oil wells and other petroleum infrastructure. Looking beyond oil, clashes between rival ethnic communities over market space have occurred in Lagos and several other states in recent years.

Political disagreements. Even at the local level, Nigerian politics is a high-stakes, winner-take-all contest for a share of the nation's petroleum revenues, lucrative government contracts, land rights, and public sector jobs. Following Nigeria's 1999 return to civilian rule, intercommunal political competition increased exponentially. In some areas, political disputes between groups that view themselves to be indigenes and those labeled non-indigenes (i.e., non-natives, settlers) have become a flashpoint of communal violence. Nowhere is this more true than in Jos, Plateau State's deeply polarized, multiethnic capital.

Jos remains a city on edge, riven with ethnopolitical divides between indigenes—the Berom, Anaguta, and Afizere people—and non-indigenes—ethnic Hausa people who migrated to the city over the past several decades to trade and work. This divide also has a religious dimension: the three indigenous groups are overwhelmingly Christian, while the Hausa are predominantly Muslim. Although almost a decade has passed since the city's last major intercommunal crisis, which left more than three hundred people dead following disputed local elections, tensions remain high. Ethnic conflict has resulted in the segregation of the city's neighborhoods by ethnicity and religion.

Beyond these three root causes, the three additional factors discussed below sustain communal conflicts, exacerbate them, and make them more difficult to resolve.

Weak and divisive governance. Local government malfeasance and the politicization of traditional leadership structures over the last four decades have undermined government's capacity to prevent and help communities recover from episodes of violence. Likewise, Nigeria's corrupt and lethargic judiciary has shown minimal capacity to resolve communal disputes. Traditional arbitration structures—such as clan chiefs or village heads—also hold less clout than ever. Divisive governance, especially at the local level, continues to stoke antipathy between rival ethnic groups in Plateau State and southern Kaduna State.

Policing failures. Under-resourced and unprofessional, the police and other security agencies rarely intervene to deter, prevent, and constructively respond to outbreaks of communal conflict. When such violence does flare up, security agencies often respond with a heavy hand, conducting hasty crackdowns that result in civilian deaths and property destruction. These reprisal operations exacerbate communal conflict in the long term by inflicting socioeconomic damage on already vulnerable communities and deepening local political grievances. In some cases, local police take sides in communal conflicts, making them more difficult to resolve or even escalating them.

Cycles of reprisal. If left unaddressed, communal conflicts can mutate into self-perpetuating cycles of violence. After years—or even decades—of tit-for-tat violence, the origins of these conflicts become less motivating than avenging past attacks. Communities locked in such cycles of violence develop a siege mentality, resulting in small arms proliferation and the creation of ethnic militias. In southern Kaduna State, for example, intercommunal clashes have erupted every few years since the late 1980s, killing thousands.

Despite the seemingly intractable nature of communal violence in Nigeria, many civil society groups, some traditional and religious leaders, and even a few government officials are working to defuse communal conflict. For example, the Interfaith Mediation Center, based in Kaduna, is a nationwide organization working at the grassroots level to mediate conflict between Christians and Muslims. Security officials in Gombe, Nasarawa, Oyo, Abia, and several other states have convened town hall meetings that bring together farmers, herders, and government officials to discuss and resolve disputes before they escalate into violence. In addition to saving lives and preventing atrocities, these types of conflict resolution efforts may also yield economic gains: a recent report estimated that Nigeria could reap up to $13.7 billion in additional productivity and revenues if farmer–herdsmen conflicts in four Middle Belt states ceased.[17]

What are the Nigerian Army's strengths and weaknesses?

In spite of its many shortcomings, the NA remains a formidable force and one of Africa's largest armies. It is actively engaged in internal security operations across the country, and it has been deployed on international peacekeeping missions since 1960. The NA is one of Nigeria's few unifying national institutions and is widely respected by Nigerians despite its past involvement in politics and its poor human rights record. Yet the force's as yet unrealized potential has been sapped by decades of corruption, mismanagement, and training and equipment shortfalls. By embracing just a few key reforms, the NA could address these nagging weaknesses and credibly claim to be a professional, world-class military force.

To understand the NA of today, however, we must first take a look at its postcolonial development. Although the NA's structure, doctrine, and organizational culture resemble those of its British colonial mentor, various historical episodes have had an even greater impact on its evolution. Foremost among these are the events of 1966 and the catastrophic civil war that followed.

Led by five revolutionary young majors from southern Nigeria, the January coup upended a civilian-led parliamentary system that they thought was corrupt and ineffective, inflamed ethnic and religious divisions within the military and across society, and marked the beginning of more than three decades of military interference in national politics.[18] Mass killings of ethnic Igbos and other southerners took place across the north, leaving thousands dead and displacing many more. A July 1966 counter-coup led by northern officers set the stage for the secession, a year later, of the self-declared state of Biafra and the prolonged and bloody civil war that followed.

By the time it ended in January 1970, the civil war had left more than one million people—mostly Biafran civilians—dead. By war's end, the ranks of the NA had expanded exponentially, from two brigades totaling 10,000 men to a 250,000-strong force made up of three divisions.[19] Following the war, the military reorganized and integrated some Biafran soldiers as part of a reconciliation policy that head of state General Yakubu Gowon described as "no victor, no vanquished." Successive military governments remained wary of the political implications of downsizing the NA, however, leaving it bloated and cash strapped throughout the 1970s.[20]

After briefly ceding power to an elected government in 1979, the military used civilian politicians' malfeasance as a pretext to reseize control in 1983. Over the next fifteen years four top army generals—Buhari, Babangida, Abacha, and Abubakar—served as head of state. During this time military officers—some relatively junior—became ministers, military administrators, and agency heads in control of multi-million-dollar budgets.[21] By the time of the 1999 civilian transition, many junior and mid-level military officers had grown used to the corrupt practices they had honed during the late 1980s and 1990s and continued to engage in them as they were promoted by successive civilian administrations.[22] Rather than being a golden age in the NA's development, this extended period of military rule left the force weakened and in need of recapitalization, reorientation, and reform.

Since Nigeria's return to civilian rule, the NA has shown little interest in snatching back the reins of government. President Obasanjo (1999–2007)—himself a former military head of state—deftly retired many officers who had held senior positions under military rule and undertook a "bureaucratization" of the military by integrating its leadership into government patronage networks. While this succeeded in keeping the military in the barracks and out of politics, it sustained the corruption and dysfunctional leadership that had for decades hobbled the NA. Among the casualties of this phenomenon was Nigeria's reputation as a capable regional and international peacekeeper. Just a few years after helping stabilize Sierra Leone and Liberia, the NA struggled to deploy peacekeepers to Darfur and Mali, and those they did send did not perform well.

Today the NA consists of eight divisions, each tasked with safeguarding a geographic area of responsibility (AOR). The country's southwest, for example, is protected by Lagos-based 81 Division and 2 Division, headquartered in Ibadan, a sprawling city that got its start less than two hundred years ago as a camp for Yoruba warriors.[23] Responsibility for protecting the country's war-torn northeast now falls to two formations, 7 Division and 8 Division, which were recently created to tackle the growing threat from Boko Haram. Patrolling the restive Niger Delta is the job of newly created 6 Division. Southeast Nigeria is Enugu-based 82 Division's bailiwick. Kaduna-based 1 Division is tasked with protecting the northwest, while Jos-headquartered 3 Division is responsible for securing the conflict-prone Middle Belt.

Divisional commanders—known as general officers commanding (GOCs)—hold the rank of major general and typically are seasoned professionals. Six of Nigeria's eight military heads of state and most chiefs of army staff at one time served as GOCs. Each division consists of up to four brigades as well as artillery, signals, engineering, and other combat support units. The average brigade consists of three battalions based in separate locations across the brigade's AOR. Usually commanded by a lieutenant colonel, battalions should consist of just under eight hundred troops, though many remain chronically understrength after sending personnel to augment units in the northeast.

Despite its impressive order of battle, the NA is in desperate need of modernization, professionalization, and institutional reform. Decades of corruption, mismanagement, and weak oversight have undermined the NA's ability to combat internal threats like Boko Haram or deploy on international peacekeeping missions. Although corruption is ubiquitous across the Nigerian security sector, the army is disproportionately affected because of its large budget, over-secretiveness, and high operational tempo. For their part, Nigeria's international military partners have done little to discourage security sector corruption, incorrectly viewing their anticorruption and counterterrorism efforts as mutually exclusive rather than complementary.[24]

Another significant weakness of the NA is its propensity to use excessive force and heavy-handed, counterproductive tactics that often result in human rights violations. While not unique to the NA—such behavior is also demonstrated by the police, other security agencies, and vigilante groups—it tarnishes the force's reputation. Such episodes of abuse also suggest that the NA sees collective punishment of civilian communities as a legitimate and effective military tactic, which it is not. Instead of holding its personnel accountable for doing so, the NA reflexively dismisses allegations of abuse, vilifies its critics, or seeks to absolve itself via internal investigations that lack transparency and objectivity and therefore credibility.

Out of the many human rights abuses allegedly committed by the NA since 1999, five major violations stand out: the 1999 destruction of the town of Odi in Bayelsa State, in which it killed hundreds of civilians after locals killed several policemen; a similar incident in 2001, in which the NA killed more than one hundred civilians in the town of Zaki Biam in Benue State; the 2009 military crackdown in Maiduguri against Mohammed Yusuf and his followers, in which up to eight hundred people—including many civilian bystanders—were killed; the deaths of several thousand detainees at the notorious Giwa Barracks and other NA-operated detention facilities from late 2011 to date; and the December 2015 massacre of more than three hundred people in the city of Zaria in Kaduna State following a clash between soldiers and members of Ibrahim Zakzaky's Shia sect, the Islamic Movement of Nigeria (IMN).

Despite its flaws and challenges, the NA has enormous potential that meaningful security sector reform and minor cultural shifts could unlock. To do so, the NA could reorganize with the aim of reducing its "tooth-to-tail" ratio, shifting resources away from administrative and noncombat support functions toward modern training, equipment, and troop welfare. Quelling interservice rivalries and improving cooperation with the Nigerian Navy and Nigerian Air Force would also help make Nigeria's military more effective.

Given that Nigeria ranks among those countries at highest risk for defense and security sector corruption, according to Transparency International, the NA has an opportunity to embrace international best practices for conducting procurement, ensuring financial transparency, and fielding much-needed management controls.[25]

The NA could also work to devolve its overly centralized decision-making away from top brass to mid-level officers at the operational level and hold them accountable for their conduct both on and off the battlefield. By embracing these and other minor reforms, the NA could mitigate some of its current weaknesses and allow its latent strengths—grit, patriotism, and fighting spirit—to take center stage.

Why are vigilantes prevalent in Nigeria?

Ndi-nche, CJTF, *yan banga*, Bakassi Boys, *olode*, hunters; Nigerian vigilante groups have a variety of colorful names but share a common purpose: combating local insecurity. With roots that can be traced back to the country's precolonial past, vigilante groups are now a widespread—albeit flawed—substitute for the anemic Nigeria Police Force (NPF). Despite being one of the world's largest unitary police forces, the 400,000-strong NPF is corrupt, poorly trained, and occasionally predatory. The NPF is mostly invisible outside Nigeria's towns and cities, except at road checkpoints, where its black-uniformed officers can be seen soliciting petty bribes from motorists.

Outgunned and under-resourced, Nigeria's police are understandably reluctant to patrol in remote, unwelcoming, or high-threat areas like parts of Borno State, the Niger Delta, or the Middle Belt. In many places vigilante groups, local militias, and the army fill the security vacuum the NPF leaves behind. Popular perceptions of vigilante groups vary, but recent field research suggests many Nigerians prefer vigilante groups to the police.[26]

Headquartered in Abuja, the NPF is led by an inspector-general of police (IGP) appointed by the president and is subordinate to the minister of the interior. The NPF consists of thirty-seven state police commands,[27] each led by a commissioner of police (CP). These state commands are grouped into geographic zonal commands overseen by an assistant inspector general of police (AIG). The NPF budget is about $1.1 billion, roughly one-third of what the London Metropolitan Police force spends annually.[28]

Unlike in the United States, Nigeria's state governments are barred by the constitution from setting up their own police forces. Police personnel are recruited nationally according to a state quota system designed to ensure the force is ethnically diverse and reflects Nigeria's "federal character." Police personnel of all ranks are redeployed every few years to both develop their career and reduce their chances of being co-opted by politicians or local criminal networks. Designed to stop police from being used as private goons, these measures have made it easier for federal officials to use the police to meddle in state politics, especially at election time.

In addition to chronic budget and manpower shortfalls and heavy-handedness in dealing with the public, Nigerian

law enforcement is handicapped by a dysfunctional judiciary, inadequate prison system, and competing agencies with
overlapping responsibilities. In addition to the NPF, Nigeria
has a panoply of nonmilitary security outfits, including the
SSS (responsible for internal security and counterterrorism),
Nigerian Security and Civil Defence Corps (civil defense),
the Federal Road Safety Commission (traffic and road safety),
Nigerian Drug Law Enforcement Agency (counternarcotics),
Economic and Financial Crimes Commission (anticorruption), Nigerian Customs Service, Nigerian Prison Service, and
Nigerian Immigration Service (border control).

Despite having a surfeit of law enforcement agencies,
Nigeria has one of the lowest incarceration rates in the world
for a country its size. Many of the country's prisons were
built during the colonial era and have been neglected and
underfunded by successive governments. All but a few are
badly overcrowded, with inmates experiencing abuse and inhumane conditions. Roughly three-quarters of all prisoners
are awaiting trial by the country's sclerotic courts, having not
yet been convicted of a crime.[29]

The speed and fairness of Nigeria's justice process is also
hampered by poor coordination between, and malfeasance by,
the federal and state entities involved: after the federal police
arrest a suspect, they detain him at a police station or remand
him in federal prison while state prosecutors and federal police investigators work together to prepare a case to take to either state or federal court. If convicted, a prison inmate might
nevertheless be pardoned at some point by the state governor.
As a result, the average pre-trial detention period in Nigeria is
3.7 years.[30]

Yet the proliferation of vigilante groups belies more than
just policing and judicial failures: it also suggests that, unlike
their uniformed predecessors, Nigeria's more recent civilian
leaders have relaxed their grip on the state's monopoly
over the use of force.[31] Free to use force with near-impunity,
vigilantes often also receive political top cover and financial

resources from state and local officials. These officials see several upsides to arming and mobilizing otherwise-unemployed youth who can moonlight as political thugs. In Rivers State, for example, the People's Democratic Party have armed and funded Ateke Tom's Niger Delta Vigilante Group as a tool for rigging elections.[32]

Once co-opted or criminalized, vigilantes can become a danger to their communities, even as they continue to defend them from external threats. In Borno State, the Civilian Joint Task Force (CJTF) vigilante group formed in 2013 as a local response to the threat of security force abuses. Well organized, armed with homemade weapons, and many thousand strong, the state-funded CJTF mobilizes poorly educated young men with few employment prospects, tasking them with identifying Boko Haram suspects, manning vehicle and pedestrian checkpoints, and guiding soldiers on rural patrols. A highly effective counterinsurgency force, the CJTF has nevertheless carried out extrajudicial killings of Boko Haram suspects, often with the tacit approval of—or in conjunction with—Nigerian security personnel.[33] It remains to be seen whether the CJTF can be gradually disarmed, demobilized, and reintegrated into civilian life or whether, as has happened with other vigilante groups across Nigeria, it embraces its darker impulses.

6

NIGERIA AND THE WORLD

Informed opinion in the United States has long concluded that Nigeria was Africa's most important country strategically. Factors cited have been its huge population, oil production, contributions to international organizations, leadership in African conflict resolution, and especially, participation in multilateral peacekeeping missions. There has also been a much darker observation that should Nigeria fail, the cause of democracy and the rule of law throughout the continent would be weakened.

Under President Obasanjo (1999–2007), Nigeria led international dispute resolution initiatives and peacekeeping in countries such as Sierra Leone and Liberia. Over the past decade, however, Nigeria's conventional international leadership has receded. Its oil has lessened in strategic importance to the United States with the rise of other producers in Africa and the Western Hemisphere. The worldwide decline in the price of oil badly damaged state finances and encouraged a retreat from international involvement. Under the Yar'Adua, Jonathan, and Buhari administrations (2007–present) the country increasingly looked inward as the state faced financial shortfalls, domestic political turmoil, and assault by the Boko Haram and Niger Delta insurgencies.

A founder and early champion of the African Union, Nigeria now plays a diminished role in the AU and other international organizations. While it led the African effort to remove a tyrannical dictator in The Gambia in 2016, its involvement has become the exception rather than the rule. Its once-active multilateral and bilateral diplomacy is now muted, with prolonged ambassadorial vacancies and serious underfunding at its missions to the UN, Washington, and London. President Jonathan's administration was particularly detrimental to Nigeria's international reputation because of rampant corruption, human rights abuses by his security services, and its slow response to the Boko Haram insurgency. Presidents Jimmy Carter, Bill Clinton, and George W. Bush all visited Nigeria. However, during his eight-year presidency President Barack Obama never did.

Yet there has been an efflorescence of Nigerian culture globally. Nigeria has a long history of international cultural influence. As the country has retreated from its role in international politics and economics, this worldwide influence in literature, film, and music has grown dramatically without either support or hindrance from the government on any level. While these cultural achievements certainly promote black and African identity, it remains to be seen what the influence will be on the development of a popular sense of identity with the Nigerian state.

How does Nigeria view its role in the world and in Africa?

During the independence period, some Nigerian elites embraced the "Nigeria project," the idea that, based in the pan-African movement, an independent, democratic Nigeria would have the heft to give Africans a seat at the world's head table. This ideal, even if never universally accepted by elites, persisted through coups, the civil war, military governments, and into the current civilian, democratic dispensation. For example, there is a near-universal belief among its opinion leaders that Nigeria would be the only appropriate permanent representative of Africa on a hypothetical, reformed UN Security

Council. Indeed, there is a belief in Nigerian "exceptionalism" that recalls that of many Americans about the United States.

After independence, successive Nigerian governments, military and civilian, were active in the full range of international organizations, including the UN General Assembly, the Commonwealth of Nations, and the World Trade Organization, among others. In addition, Nigerians sought and held high office in these organizations, and there was a significant Nigerian presence in technical and administrative positions. Within Africa, Nigeria played the lead role in the establishment of the fifteen-state ECOWAS and hosts its headquarters in Abuja. It also provides the lion's share of the ECOWAS budget and most of its civil servants. Nigeria also played the lead role in the transformation of the OAU into the AU, to reflect Africa's postcolonial reality after the dismantling of apartheid in South Africa.

Nigeria has an able diplomatic service supported by a diplomatic training facility, and Nigerian think-tanks (notably the Nigeria Institute of International Affairs) that provide subject matter expertise. Nigeria maintains embassies in almost every country in the world. In fact, the number of Nigerian diplomatic establishments is approximately the same as that of the United States. The Nigerian diplomatic service has many female members, some of whom are ambassadors. Rare in Africa, there have been two female Nigerian foreign ministers in recent memory, Joy Ogwu and Ngozi Okonjo-Iweala.

Nigerian elites assume their country is the "hegemon" of West Africa. Other Africans regularly accuse Nigerians of being boastful, overbearing, and arrogant. As the presumed leader of the continent, they traditionally view with suspicion the ongoing role of France in its former West African possessions. (All of Nigeria's land borders are with small, francophone states.) Similarly, Nigeria's military has been hesitant about close collaboration with foreign—especially American—militaries operating on the continent, particularly in West Africa. Every civilian government has been suspicious of the

United States Africa Command (AFRICOM). When the United States refuses to supply the military equipment Abuja wants, usually on the basis of persistent human rights violations by its security services, Nigeria readily turns to Russia and China as alternative suppliers.

On the African continent, Nigeria's relationship with South Africa has been ambiguous. Apartheid South Africa was the national enemy during the post-independence and civil war periods, and Nigeria actively supported the African National Congress (ANC) and other anti-apartheid movements. In turn, the white, apartheid National Party government in Pretoria supported the cause of independent Biafra. After he resigned as military chief of state but before he was elected president in 1999, Obasanjo was personally involved in Commonwealth and other multilateral initiatives to persuade the apartheid government to step down. Since the end of apartheid, the two countries have been rivals for influence on the African continent, despite protestations of friendship and cooperation. Far from conceding continent-wide leadership to Nigeria, South Africa also argues that it would be the most appropriate African state to serve as a permanent member of a reformed UN Security Council.

Nigeria's relationship with China, now the world's second largest economy, is also ambiguous. China views Africa as an important source of oil and gas but arrived late to the industry in Nigeria. There have been talks—even bilateral agreements—that would exchange Nigerian oil for Chinese infrastructure projects, but only a handful have come to fruition. Nigeria is, however, a major market for Chinese manufactured goods and has a trade deficit with the Asian nation, a rare situation for an oil-exporting country to be in. For Nigeria, what is perhaps more important than economic considerations is China's role as an alternative political and diplomatic partner to the West, especially the United Kingdom and the United States.

Despite media attention to its real or potential economic relationship with China, the countries of the European Union remain a major source of foreign investment in Nigeria, and some provide significant development assistance. They are also a major source of imports and a growing market for Nigerian oil and gas. Bilateral and multilateral diplomatic relations are warm. Nigeria's ties to Russia are much less important than those with Europe, China, and the United States, particularly because Russia is a major producer of oil and gas and therefore not a market for Nigeria's principal export. Nor is Russia a major source of imports, with the exception of weapons and military equipment.

Nigeria's economic ties to India and South Asia are strengthening, especially as the market for oil and natural gas grows. There has been a small, well-adapted South Asian population in Nigeria since colonial times, and Indian businesspeople play an important entrepreneurial role. They appear to be well integrated into the Nigerian business community, make use of local labor, and do not engender the same hostility from Nigerians that Chinese tend to do.

At present, Nigeria's role in the world is constrained by its shortage of leadership and institutional capacity. Especially when oil prices are low, diplomats, like other civil servants, can go for long periods without pay, and their recruitment and training atrophies. Furthermore, "federal character," with its mandate that high level positions be distributed equitably among the states, makes ambassadorial appointments cumbersome. The Ministry of Foreign Affairs often has little scope in authority because the presidency (the "Villa") frequently conducts Nigerian diplomacy directly. Strong leaders such as President Obasanjo (1999–2007) serve as their own foreign ministers in fact if not in title. Obasanjo, for example, personally negotiated the resolution of a territorial dispute over the Bakassi peninsula with Cameroonian head of state Paul Biya. He also carefully tended the bilateral relationship with the United States. For example, he was the first African head of state to pay a condolence call on President George W. Bush in the aftermath of 9/11.

What are Nigeria's relations like with Washington and London?

Nigeria regards its relations with the United States and the United Kingdom as its most important outside of Africa, and characterized by partnership, not patronage. In Washington and London, Nigeria's ambassador (US) and high commissioner (UK) are always political appointees and are usually important personages in their own right. London and Washington, in turn, usually regard Abuja as their most important African diplomatic posting. The American ambassador and the British high commissioner are almost always senior career members of their respective diplomatic services.

Elites in Nigeria take pride in their country's membership in the Commonwealth of Nations. The country periodically hosts the Commonwealth Heads of Government Meeting (CHOGM), the organization's consulting and decision-making body, and Nigerian Emeka Anyaoku served as Commonwealth secretary general from 1990 to 2000. In addition to its embassies in Washington and to the United Nations in New York, from time to time Nigeria has maintained consulates in Atlanta, Chicago, Houston, Los Angeles, Miami, and San Francisco.

The American diplomatic presence in Nigeria consists of an embassy in Abuja and a consulate in Lagos. In the past the United States maintained consulates in Enugu, Ibadan, Kaduna, and Kano, with the embassy in Lagos. The consulates were closed, largely for budgetary reasons, and the embassy moved to Abuja after then head of state Babangida established it as the working (rather than symbolic) federal capital and directed foreign embassies to move there in 1991. (The former embassy in Lagos was transformed into a consulate at that time.) The Obama administration (2009–2017) planned to open an additional consulate in Kano, but the Boko Haram insurrection raised security concerns that precluded that step.

As Nigeria is a member of the Commonwealth, its embassy in London is called a high commission. The United Kingdom reciprocally maintains a high commission in Abuja and a deputy high commission in Lagos. The United Kingdom once had an extensive network of diplomatic establishments throughout the country, but they have been progressively reduced, again because of budget constraints. However, the British Council, an independent but government-funded entity involved in cultural and exchange activities, has offices in Abuja, Kano, Lagos, and Port Harcourt. Despite the cutbacks, the American and British diplomatic establishments are the largest in Nigeria, and a large percentage of senior Nigerian diplomats have served in the United Kingdom or the United States at some point during their careers.

While Nigeria is the venue of the largest American investment in Africa, it is primarily in only one industry, petrochemicals. British investments, though in total smaller, are considerably more diversified. Among Nigerian elites, the United Kingdom remains the purveyor of choice of luxury goods and the venue of choice for educational and medical services.

Diplomatic relations have their ups and downs, often driven by Nigerian domestic developments. For example, following a 1984 Nigerian effort to kidnap from London Umaru Dikko, a disgraced former politician accused of corruption, the then military government's bilateral relationship with the United Kingdom cooled for several years. When in 2014 Washington declined to sell certain military materiel to Nigeria, Abuja reacted with anger. Cordiality was largely restored under Buhari, though Nigerian elite resentment remains over restrictive US arms sales policies.

In 1979 Obasanjo's military government nationalized British Petroleum (BP)'s Nigerian operations and holdings. His motivation appears to have been to punish the Thatcher government for its policies toward then apartheid South Africa and white-ruled Rhodesia. Moreover, Obasanjo's government viewed BP as a colonial vestige, in part because the British government owned a significant percentage of its shares at that time. (Shell, usually Nigeria's largest oil producer, is headquartered in London and The Hague, but the British government did not own any shares.)

A recurring complication in bilateral relationships is the American and British visa regime. With the myriad ties between Nigeria and the United Kingdom and the United States, there are many official and elite Nigerian travelers wanting to travel among the three countries. But Nigerians have a reputation for visa fraud and abuse. As a consequence, a significant percentage of visa applicants are denied. Nigerians often view the visa application process as onerous and infused with racism. Until 2006, Nigerians had to travel to Lagos to apply for an American visa. Now they may also apply in Abuja.

Is China a big player in Nigeria?

China is a player in Nigeria, but not to the same extent as it is elsewhere in Africa. There have been Chinese in Nigeria since the colonial period. Scattered all over the country are Chinese restaurants, favored by elites for a celebratory night out. Chinese of Hong Kong and Taiwanese origin constitute their own communities and are distinct from those involved with the post-1949 Beijing regime. Those Chinese communities that date from the colonial period have long been involved in business, both large and small, and are better integrated than the Beijing Chinese community, which arrived more recently.

Though statistics are weak, there are an estimated two million Chinese nationals in Africa, only a small percentage of whom are in Nigeria. In 1999 it was estimated that there were 5,800 Chinese in Nigeria, of whom 1,050 were from Hong Kong and 630 were from Taiwan.[1] That number has almost certainly grown during the past decade, though from a small base.

Conversely, there is a large Nigerian community living in China, almost certainly larger than the Chinese population in Nigeria. One estimate is that in 2012 there were 500,000 Africans in China, of whom the largest portion by far was

Nigerian.[2] Anecdotal evidence indicates that Nigerians in China are mostly businesspersons and students, and most do not stay long. As is frequently the case for other immigrant communities around the world, Nigerians in China appear primarily to be students and traders.

During the civil war Beijing favored Biafra, apparently largely because its archrival at the time, the Soviet Union, favored the federal government. Lagos, in turn, maintained diplomatic relations with Taiwan. However, after the end of the civil war Lagos, seeing the potential for greater international influence, set aside its pique over Biafra and recognized Beijing, breaking formal diplomatic ties with Taiwan. Perhaps in return, Beijing publicly supported Nigeria for a permanent seat on a reformed UN Security Council, a symbolic gesture that had little practical consequence. The "transactional" nature of the bilateral relationship continues; in 2017, following a Chinese pledge of up to $40 billion in infrastructure investment in Nigeria, the Buhari administration ordered the Taiwanese to close their trade office in Abuja and move to Lagos, thereby further minimizing official ties to Taiwan.

Especially over the past decade, the Nigeria–China bilateral political and diplomatic relationship has become more important as Beijing increases its engagement with Africa. For its part, Nigeria hopes to be Africa's chief interlocutor with China. Each views the other as a useful counterbalance to the West. Hence, when the West cold-shouldered China in the aftermath of the 1989 Chinese massacre of pro-democracy demonstrators at Tiananmen Square, Beijing warmed up its ties with Nigeria and other countries in the developing world. Similarly, during the dark days of Sani Abacha, when Nigeria was a pariah and suspended from the Commonwealth, the Abacha government turned to Beijing. More recently, when the United States declined to sell weaponry to Abuja because of persistent human rights violations, the Jonathan administration turned to Moscow, while the Buhari government looked to Beijing.

China's role in Nigeria and the quality of the bilateral relationship remains ambiguous. On the one hand, a 2014 BBC poll showed that 85 percent of Nigerians viewed China's world role as positive, making Nigeria the world's most pro-Chinese country. On the other hand, cheap Chinese imports have contributed to the collapse of Nigeria's manufacturing and industrial sectors. The value of bilateral trade increased from $384 million in 1998 to $3 billion in 2006.[3] Nevertheless, the balance of trade strongly favors China. Between 2013 and 2015, China sold to Nigeria 7.8 times as much as it imported.[4]

China's state-owned oil companies started to enter the Nigerian oil market in a big way only in 2005, when they acquired a stake in an oil block from a Nigerian producer. They have sought more assets since then, though with limited success. The Chinese government has financed—and Chinese companies have undertaken—important infrastructure projects, notably the restoration of a railway system. These projects are not as extensive, however, as in other parts of Africa. Intended high-profile investments in the Nigerian oil sector often run aground on the government's requirement that foreign investors have equal Nigerian partners.

Complaints about the Chinese in Nigeria are similar to those found elsewhere in Africa: the Chinese are "racist" insofar as they do not make use of local labor, and they do not establish a career ladder for Nigerian employees. In general, there is little transfer of skills or technology between the Chinese and Nigerians.

Does Nigeria have a human rights problem?

Human rights issues in Nigeria highlight the dichotomy between aspiration and reality. With the notable exception of lesbian, gay, and transgendered people, Nigerian laws provide the full spectrum of human rights guarantees. Moreover, Nigeria has also signed and ratified the major international human rights agreements. The reality, however, is very different. Weak state capacity, official corruption, poverty, and religious divisions severely limit the free exercise of many fundamental human rights.

As has been the case since the colonial period, Nigerians are largely alienated from the security services, including the military and police. In turn, the security services are undertrained, underfunded, and relatively few in number. Their abuses continue to help drive recruitment for Boko Haram. For its part, Boko Haram and other similar movements altogether reject the concept of human rights and violate international norms with impunity. In particular, they target members of the security services and others associated with the secular state.

Multiple legal systems and a sclerotic and often corrupt judiciary means that justice is nearly always delayed and often denied. That encourages individuals and mobs to take justice into their own hands; a mob in a market, for example, may capture and summarily kill an alleged thief. The security services will also take justice into their own hands. A notorious example is the 2009 extrajudicial killing of Mohammed Yusuf, then the leader of Boko Haram, by police. If police arrest a suspect (as opposed to killing him outright), that suspect faces a long wait in an overcrowded and inhumane prison before being brought to trial.

The US Department of State's annual human rights report on Nigeria—a credible and painstakingly researched document—finds violations in virtually every one of its categories. These reports exhaustively record human rights violations involving arbitrary or unlawful deprivation of life, disappearance, torture, and arbitrary arrest. While many of the violations are by terrorist groups like Boko Haram, others are perpetrated by state entities. There are similar reports from numerous human rights–focused NGOs.[5]

The constitution proclaims that Nigeria is a secular state with absolute freedom of religion. However, Christian and Muslim holidays are observed, and the state funds with public money pilgrimages to Mecca and Jerusalem. Sharia law legally operates in the criminal domain in twelve northern states, seemingly in contradiction to the constitution. Though it is supposed to apply only to Muslims, sharia's reach can extend to Christians, such as in matters of inheritance and other aspects of family law. Homosexual activity has long been criminalized by both major religions; a 2013 Pew Global Attitudes Project reported that 98 percent of Nigerians believed that homosexuality is unacceptable.[6] Unsurprisingly then, a law prohibiting gay marriage passed with support from Christians and Muslims in 2013 and included draconian penalties. Though these have been minimally enforced, the threat hangs over the head of homosexuals across Nigeria.

Laws to protect women and children are on the books, notably the 2003 Child Rights Act, which prohibits marriage below the age of eighteen and outlaws forms of child labor. Yet in northern Nigeria, the average age of marriage for women is between fourteen and fifteen, and children everywhere work. The United Nations Children's Fund (UNICEF) estimates that 40 percent of Nigerian children age six to eleven do not attend school. While this statistic reflects a shortage of educational facilities, family poverty also drives child labor and absence from school. Especially in the north, educational discrimination against girls is widespread. If it must choose, a poor family will favor education for boys over girls. Anecdotally, rape is pervasive across the country while punishment is rare, reflecting a widespread lack of value for women and girls.[7]

Similarly, while there are laws that guarantee freedom of expression and of the press, these are poorly enforced. The Committee to Protect Journalists has reported official intimidation and violence against individuals and newspapers that published stories unfavorable to the government. More locally, "big men" will use violence to intimidate the media. Law enforcement and the judiciary are chronically underfunded and are generally ambivalent about protecting press freedoms.[8]

In the second decade of the twenty-first century, human rights in Nigeria are suspended between aspiration and reality. The country aspires to the full realization of these rights, but its profoundly conservative society and lack of institutional and bureaucratic capacity ensure that this remains only an aspiration.

Where is the Nigerian diaspora, and why is it so influential?

The UN estimates that 1.2 million Nigerians live outside their home country. Hard data are not available, but other unconfirmed estimates, often based on Nigerian social media, range from five to fifteen million.[9] The higher figures tend to include the children born outside Nigeria to Nigerian parents who continue to identify as Nigerian. Among those Nigerians who leave West Africa, the most common destinations are the United Kingdom, the United States, China, and South Africa. As of 2015, about 376,000 Nigerians lived in the United States, heavily concentrated in New York and Houston.[10] That figure is almost certainly too low, and it does not include many undocumented immigrants. The UK official figure was 191,000, with the same caveats.

The Nigerian community in the United States is relatively prosperous. According to the Migration Policy Institute, its family median annual income was $52,000 in 2015, and Nigerians rank among the most educated immigrant groups in the United States. The World Bank estimates that in 2012 Nigerians in the United States alone remitted about $6.1 billion home, out of a total of $21.6 billion in remittances to Nigeria that year.[11]

The current diaspora has accelerated since 1990 and continues to drain the country of young, highly educated Nigerians. Celebrated cultural luminaries such as the Nobel playwright Wole Soyinka (*The Swamp Dwellers*) and Booker Prize–winning author Chinua Achebe (*Things Fall Apart*), who both lived in the United States for many years, were part of this movement. Others continue to travel back and forth. The author Chimamanda Ngozi Adichie (*Half of a Yellow Sun*) divides her time between Nigeria and the United States. The rapper Jidenna was born in the United States to a Nigerian mother and an American father, spending a portion of his childhood in Nigeria before returning to Massachusetts.

In the United States and the United Kingdom, medical professionals figure prominently among Nigerian expatriates. In 2013 the president of the Nigeria Medical Association estimated that of 71,740 medical doctors registered with the Medical and Dental Council, only 27,000 were actually practicing in Nigeria. He said that some 7,000 Nigerian medical doctors work in public health in the United Kingdom and the United States. In addition, thousands of other medical professionals from Nigeria, like nurses and pharmacists, have moved away to Europe and the Western Hemisphere.[12]

The Nigerian diaspora plays an important role in helping modern expressions of Nigerian culture reach an international audience. The diaspora in the United Kingdom has been particularly influential in popularizing and adapting Nigerian pop music, like Afro-beat and grime. Especially in the case of the latter, this music incorporated social protest and reflected the identity crisis experienced by second-generation African immigrants. The Nigerian diaspora in other parts of Africa has played an important role in developing the market for what is now a multi-billion-dollar Nigerian film industry, generally called Nollywood.

In the fine arts, there is a high level of cross-fertilization between the diaspora and Nigerians at home. Art critics see the paintings of such prominent Nigerian artists as Ben Osaghae and the photographs of Adolphus Opara as helping to shape a Nigerian postcolonial identity. As with Nigerian literature, however, the market for Nigerian fine art is larger abroad than it is at home.

The Nigerian diaspora and their children have produced outstanding professional athletes in the United States and the United Kingdom. Examples include brothers Samuel and Emmanuel Acho in the National Football League and sisters Nneka and Chiney Ogwumike in the Women's National Basketball Association. Christian Okoye was a football running back with the Kansas City Chiefs, while Hakeem Olajuwon enjoyed a basketball career with the Houston Rockets that led to his 2008 induction into the Basketball Hall of Fame. In the United Kingdom there have been numerous Nigerian soccer (football) players, including Alex Iwobifor and Nwankwo Kanu for Arsenal and Victor Moses and Celestine Babayaro for Chelsea.

The diaspora in the United States has also been an important transmitter of Nigerian approaches to Christianity. One Nigerian denomination, the Redeemed Christian Church of God (RCCG), claims to have established 720 churches with fifteen thousand members across the United States. It is Pentecostal in its form of worship, and while most of its members in the United States are Africans, it is actively reaching out to Americans from outside the African diaspora.

During the commodities boom of the 2000s, some Nigerians in the diaspora returned home, bringing with them their skills and expertise acquired in the United States, notably Ngozi Okonjo-Iweala of the World Bank, who became a minister in two administrations, and Oscar N. Onyema, a twenty-year veteran of US financial markets and, since 2011, the chief executive officer of the Lagos stock exchange. Nigerians who have found success in the United States are often concerned with "giving back" to Nigeria. They will often spend a few weeks or months every year pursuing their professions in Nigeria. Especially in the medical field, Nigerians practicing in the United States remain in close touch with their co-professionals at home. For example, diaspora medical doctors in the United States greatly assisted the Lagos State ministry of health in containing an outbreak of Ebola in 2014.

How does Nigeria contribute to world culture?

Even as Nigeria's international political and economic importance has declined in the second decade of the twenty-first century, its cultural influence has grown, both in Africa and overseas. Especially in film and music, Nigeria has led the way toward creating a postcolonial, African cultural identity altogether separate and apart from that of its former colonial masters. Nigeria's cultural influence on the continent, already great, is growing rapidly.

In sports, Nigeria's international reach is largely restricted to soccer. Nigeria's national team, the Super Eagles, has qualified for five of the last six FIFA world cups. The team comprises representatives of many ethnic groups. In a period of surging ethnic and religious strife, the Super Eagles are an important affirmation of Nigerian national identity and unity. Pictures of Nigerian players in many European premier league teams, including Arsenal and Chelsea, are displayed in public places—such as on the sides of buses—across sub-Saharan Africa.

Other games, notably *nambe* boxing, cricket, and wrestling, have large—albeit mostly domestic—audiences. Nambe boxing is particularly important to northern Nigeria. Predating the arrival of Islam, it incorporates many ritual elements from African traditional religion, as well as martial arts and boxing. Unlike other sports in Nigeria, it is never televised, in part because of its quasi-religious dimension, and also because its fans are mostly poor without ready access to media. In Igboland, wrestling plays a similar role in affirming and cultivating local culture, and it, too, includes religious and mystical elements. A wrestling match may even be used to resolve disputes between neighboring villages. Though there are national federations for boxing and wrestling, both sports are largely unregulated.

There are two UNESCO-designated world heritage sites in Nigeria, and another eight are on a "tentative" list. In 1999 Sukur Cultural Landscape in Adamawa State—some of which dates to the Iron Age—became the first designated heritage site. Located in the Mandara Mountains, it features terraced fields, a traditional palace, and many species of rare birds and other animals. The second is the Osun Osogbo Sacred Grove, an ancient, sacred forest associated with Yoruba traditional religion, located in Osun State. It boasts shrines to the goddess of fertility and sanctuaries sacred to other Yoruba gods. Those on the tentative list include the medieval city walls of Kano, a group of carved, monolithic stones in the Cross River State, and a statue of a warrior god in Abia State. With the exception of Osogbo (not far from Lagos) and Kano (the second largest city in the country), foreigners rarely visit Nigeria's designated and tentative UNESCO world heritage sites, a consequence of the country's underdeveloped tourist infrastructure.

Nigeria is rightly celebrated for its contribution to modern literature. In their work, authors of the independence generation, notably Chinua Achebe and Wole Soyinka, addressed the confluence of the traditional African world and their European occupiers during the colonial and early independence periods. For them, the result of that largely painful confrontation was the emergence of modern Nigeria. However, the authors' audience has always been largely European and North American, books are too expensive for most Nigerians. A second generation of Nigerian writers—Teju Cole and Chimamanda Adichie, among many others—has moved beyond colonialism and baleful European influences. Instead, they relate Nigerian themes to broader questions of "blackness" and protest politics in the countries in which they live, as well as in Nigeria. Many of the most prominent continue to explore themes related to Biafra and the Nigerian Civil War.

However, the publishing industry is weak and copyright protection hardly exists as a practical matter, limiting the size of the domestic audience. Only a handful of bookshops exist in the conventional sense to serve the entire country. This drives Nigerian authors to look for publishers abroad and in some cases to expatriate. What's more, there is anecdotal evidence that English comprehension is declining among younger Nigerians and is not being replaced with a similarly universal language. Not only does this increase the cost of reaching more Nigerians, but it also makes the English-language works of great Nigerian authors less accessible to fellow Nigerians.

The reach of film, on the other hand, is growing. Often made in Yoruba and Pidgin English as well as standard English, films are linguistically more accessible and more relevant to younger Nigerians, not to mention much less expensive to distribute than books. The domestic filmmaking industry, called Nollywood, is a significant driver of Nigeria's economy. In 2013 it produced 1,844 movies. According to the Nigerian government, Nollywood was a $3.3 billion industry in 2014, and the United States International Trade Commission estimates that it contributes $600 million to the economy every year. Furthermore, the government estimates that the industry employs one million Nigerians. All such statistics should be taken with a grain of salt, but they do indicate that Nollywood has become an economic powerhouse.

Nollywood is entirely indigenous; the industry receives no government subsidies at home or assistance from abroad, unlike cinema in francophone Africa, which often benefits from subsidies from Paris. Nevertheless, in an effort to extend the reach of Nollywood, the Nigerian Ministry of Information has begun to lobby the Beijing government to allow screenings of Nollywood films in China.

The industry is dominated by Yorubas and is centered in Lagos. Production is highly decentralized and free of any regulation. It makes use of audiovisual equipment that was introduced into Nigeria by ubiquitous film pirates. The movies are cheap to make, with budgets typically in the area of $12,000, and are filmed with basic equipment. DVD versions of Nollywood films can be purchased for a few dollars in a market. Families or villages will watch the film together on the best DVD player available to them. Formal cinemas in the Western sense hardly exist in Nigeria.

Nollywood production values are low by Western standards, but the plots and themes directly relate to the daily lives of the audiences, both in Nigeria and across sub-Saharan Africa. Nollywood plots usually overshadow the actors, though stars do exist. Films are easy to export, though like other forms of intellectual property they are often pirated; the World Bank estimates that nine copies of a film are pirated for every one that is legitimately sold. This accounts in part for the widely varying estimates of the size of Nollywood's audience. Unlike Nigerian literature or music, there is as yet little market for Nollywood in the United States and the United Kingdom outside the African expatriate community.[13]

The Nigerian music industry, unlike those of film and literature, has a strong presence both at home and abroad. It dominates the export of African music to the United States and the United Kingdom and is an integral part of the music scene in Africa. Influenced by the American Black Power movement, Fela Kuti (1938–1997) developed Afro-beat, a musical form that incorporates elements from jazz, pop, and indigenous rhythms. Fela Kuti's music had a strong protest element focused on Nigeria's military rulers. In Nigeria he established a commune and a nightclub called The Shrine. Though he came from a family of Anglican Christians, he sought to revive traditional Yoruba religion, incorporating its themes and spirituality into his music. He strongly opposed the military governments of the time, and his album *Zombie*, which satirized the military, was an international hit. In retaliation, the military burned down his commune and defenestrated his mother, who later died of her injuries.

Afro-beats (with an *s*) emerged out of Afro-beat, abandoning its protest edge and becoming international in its audience and performers. Grime, especially associated with Nigerian expatriates living in the United Kingdom, incorporates American hip-hop and Jamaican dance hall elements. Afro-beats and grime both emerged from the Nigerian diaspora abroad, eventually becoming very popular in Nigeria and elsewhere in Africa.

7

NIGERIA OF THE FUTURE

What does Nigeria's future hold? Will spiraling population growth, unchecked urban expansion, and the negative effects of climate change hold the country back? Or will technological innovation, better governance, and a more empowered and engaged citizenry take it to new heights? As complex and dynamic as Nigeria is today, it nevertheless offers us some clues about how the Nigeria of tomorrow might look.

How are Nigerian cities evolving?

In terms of size, density, and surface area, Nigeria's cities are growing rapidly. The share of Nigeria's population living in urban areas increased from roughly 30 percent in 1990 to about 50 percent in 2017; by 2050, 67 percent of all Nigerians will live in cities.[1] This booming growth has exacerbated long-standing challenges like youth unemployment, income inequality, violent crime, air and water pollution, traffic congestion, and disputes between recent migrants and longtime residents. Riddled with corruption and mismanagement, state and local governments appear incapable of adequately addressing these issues. Yet rather than becoming postmodern dystopias, Nigeria's cities most likely will remain places where a cross section of its citizens—rich and poor, strangers and locals, indolent officials and innovative entrepreneurs—uneasily coexist.

The physical expansion of Nigerian cities means shifting rural–urban boundaries are perpetually being redefined. Cities often spill across two or more local government areas and lack discrete political boundaries or unitary governance structures such as mayors or city councils. The surface area of the northern city of Kano, for example, more than doubled between 1986 and 2015.[2] As a result of this expansion, the line between urban and rural areas has blurred. Rural livelihoods have been indelibly impacted as encroaching suburbs engulf farmland, livestock grazing areas, and even whole villages. This in turn has sparked rural land disputes as displaced farmers and herders compete for open space. State officials have further aggravated these disputes by selling off undeveloped land near cities or giving it away to their political cronies.

Urban growth is not only redefining the periphery of Nigeria's cities, it is also fueling state governments' and private developers' desire to demolish centrally located slums built on what is now considered prime real estate. In theory, such demolitions are the first step toward the redevelopment and revitalization of impoverished neighborhoods. In practice, however, officials make little or no effort to resettle and rehouse the people they evict. In late 2016 and early 2017, for example, police, hired thugs, and bulldozers descended on Otodo Gbame—a waterfront slum in Lagos—killing at least eleven people and displacing thousands more.[3] Earlier clearances had decimated Makoko, an informal settlement perched on stilts in Lagos lagoon, in 2010 and 2012.[4] In Port Harcourt, officials seeking to dismantle the city's informal waterfront first tried to stigmatize the residents, claiming that "there is an awful stench that hangs in the air, and those who spend some time there carry this odor around town, giving off a whiff of decay."[5] Even in Nigeria's capital, Abuja, government demolitions have displaced several hundred thousand low-income residents over the last two decades.[6]

Urbanization has also aggravated problems of political representation and participation. Most city dwellers are ineligible to vote locally or enroll their children in public schools because they are non-indigenes; they are economic migrants from neighboring local government areas or other states. While some have acquired "certificates of origin" (indigene certificates) through marriage or at the discretion of corruption-prone local government officials, discrimination against non-indigenes is the norm.[7] Many urban migrants cope with this discrimination by making frequent visits to their home area, retaining households there, and hoping that they can eventually return or retire there with savings earned by working in the city.[8]

Looking ahead, new technology may make life a little easier for Nigerian city dwellers. The use of simple off-grid solar power systems, for example, is rapidly increasing all across Africa. If sustained, the growing use of these stand-alone connections will soon outpace the rate at which people are being connected to Nigeria's anemic electrical grid.[9] Such systems could also power pumps for borehole wells, alleviating chronic water shortages in cities like Lagos, which uses 724 million gallons of water daily, yet produces only 317 million gallons.[10] Likewise, the continued proliferation of mobile Internet technology could increase the number of Nigerians who telecommute, a trend that could make traffic in Lagos—still the largest city in the world without a mass transit system—a little less horrendous.[11] Mobile app–enabled ride-sharing and taxi services like Uber—already available in Lagos and Abuja—could also expand Nigerians' transportation options.

Will social media and information technology transform Nigerian politics, governance, and society?

Nigerians have embraced the latest information technology and modes of communication in ways that will have an outsized impact on the country's political and socioeconomic future. With smartphones become cheaper and more capable, every day Nigerians are increasingly online, searching out information; sharing ideas; and doing business across geographic, social, and cultural barriers. As they become more networked, Nigerians almost certainly will become more engaged with their governing elites, holding them accountable for their promises and actions. Even so, opportunistic politicians and their followers could also misuse social media to inflame religious and ethnic tensions and harass opponents.

Nigeria's online population is huge, active, and growing (see table 7.1). One reason is the growing affordability and improved connectivity of Internet-enabled mobile telephones. Nigeria will have an estimated ninety-five million smartphone users by 2019.[12] More than 80 percent of all web pages visited by Nigerians are accessed from mobile phones, one of the highest rates in the world.[13] As more and more mobile users have acquired smartphones with Internet access and social networking apps, the percentage of Nigerians using Internet cafés—a popular means of going online just five years ago—has plummeted to near zero.[14]

Internet use varies starkly among Nigerians, especially by education level. In a 2014 poll, 62 percent of Nigerians with a postsecondary education reported going online in the previous week, compared to 38 percent of those with a secondary education and just 8 percent of those without one.[15] Likewise, rural Nigerians enjoy far less connectivity than urban dwellers, who already experience some of the lowest Internet connection speeds in the world (below 3Mbps on average).[16]

Table 7.1 Internet, Social Media, and Mobile Telephone Usage in Nigeria

	Internet Users	Active Social Media Users	Mobile Phone Subscriptions	Active Mobile Social Users
Total	97.2 million	18.0 million	157.7 million	15.0 million
Penetration	51%	10%	83%*	8%

Source: We Are Social and Hootsuite, *2017 Digital Yearbook* (January 2017).

* The actual penetration rate is almost certainly lower, as the average mobile user owns at least two SIM cards.

Nigeria has more than sixteen million Facebook users. The photo-sharing app Instagram and the Internet telephone tool WhatsApp—both owned by Facebook—are also popular among the country's digitally savvy. In 2016 Facebook CEO Mark Zuckerberg visited Lagos, stopping in at the Co-Creation Hub, a local tech incubator, as well as meeting with digital entrepreneurs and Nollywood filmmakers. About the embryonic Nigerian tech industry, the billionaire investor and philanthropist said: "The energy here is amazing and I'm excited to learn as much as I can."[17] Zuckerberg and other investors' interest indicates that even as the country's technology, communications, and media sectors have expanded rapidly in recent years, a lot of room remains for further growth.

Though not as widely used as Facebook, Twitter has become an important venue for politically minded Nigerians to trumpet their views, debate the latest headlines, and engage—at times heatedly—with one another. Nigerians tweeted 350 million times in 2015, two and one-half times more than Kenyans and Ghanaians combined.[18] With 1.8 million registered members, online forum Nairaland remains popular, even though it has earned the nickname "Angryland" for its insult-laced political discussion threads.

During the 2015 elections both major parties, their supporters, and even state-level candidates themselves used social media to generate support and denigrate their opponents. "I think this election was decided, dominated and directed by social media," asserted Sunday Dare, a journalist and media adviser to Nigeria's ruling APC party.[19] After the vote, citizen poll observers deterred election rigging by tweeting out results posted at individual polling units and local collation centers. "Social media is now a powerful tool to protect democracy . . . [and] an important means of electioneering and policing election results," observed social activist turned journalist Audu Liberty Oseni.[20]

Twitter has also given voice (280 characters at a time) to a new generation of politically savvy "Twitterati" like Japtheth

Omojuwa (@Omojuwa), Tolu Ogunlesi (@toluogunlesi), Yadomah Mandara (@Yadomah), Onye Nkuzi (@cchukudebelu), and many others. Yet Twitter also lays bare—and some might argue exacerbates—Nigeria's deepening regional and ethno-religious political divides. Despite this worrisome trend, "*Naija Twitter*" nevertheless remains a broadly cross-cultural and polyglot medium, with tweets frequently peppered with Pidgin, Hausa, Yoruba, and Igbo phrases.

Despite operating in the shadow of Silicon Valley giants, several homegrown Internet platforms are also popular in Nigeria. Old-school discussion forum site Nairaland remains vibrant. YouTube sensation IrokoTV wants to be Nollywood's answer to Netflix. E-commerce trailblazers Jumia and Konga sell everything from spaghetti to sports equipment. Several online-only news platforms such as Premium Times, Naij.com, and Sahara Reporters now rival the readership of Nigeria's print and television news media.[21] Among civic organizations, BudgIt is distinguishing itself by leveraging technology, data visualization, and crowdsourcing to empower Nigerians by sharing information on federal and state budgets, spending, and project implementation as widely as possible.

As digital development and new media are increasing outside pressure on government to be more transparent, responsive, accountable, and accessible, a few innovative insiders are embracing social media and information sharing on their own. Dr. Joe Abah (@DrJoeAbah), erstwhile head of the Bureau of Public Service Reforms in the Office of the Presidency, became somewhat of a Twitter celebrity as he walked Nigerians through his efforts to remediate the country's anemic and venal bureaucracy. Tweeting from the corridors of power, he reliably replied to Nigerians who encounter unhelpful officials or byzantine rules, even providing guidance to those struggling to renew a driver's license or passport. Like Abah, the Economic and Financial Crimes Commission's articulate but anonymous Twitter handler (@OfficialEFCC) is an effective, engaging, and even witty voice for the agency tasked with combating government corruption. Dr. Yemi Kale (@sgyemikale), director-general of the Nigerian Bureau of Statistics, is another dynamic Twitter presence, using hard numbers to inform policy discussions and showing how statistical data affect people's everyday lives.

This looming digital transformation of governance, politics, and society is not without its obstacles, however. Broadly speaking, the Nigerian government is conservative, paper-pushing, and—like bureaucracies everywhere—suspicious of innovation and change. Many civil servants are standoffish and instinctively opaque, a behavioral product of decades of military rule, petty corruption, and unmet or delayed salary payments. Few government agencies proactively share with the public information about their activities, policies, or procurement activities. There are some signs, however, that this dynamic may change; some government agencies—most notably Nigeria's pension (@PTADNigeria) and road safety agencies (@FRSCNigeria)—are cutting red tape and using new tools to interface directly with citizens.

Although Nigeria has a free and vibrant press, security agencies still occasionally arrest journalists or social media lights accused of antagonizing powerful elites. For example, police in Lagos recently detained social activist and entrepreneur Audu Maikori for comments he made on social media about communal violence in southern Kaduna State that upset its powerful governor.[22] Similarly, in 2014 the SSS arrested a man for live-tweeting a breakout attempt by detainees held at the agency's Abuja headquarters, holding him until fellow Twitter users launched an online campaign demanding his release.[23]

Despite these incidents, the Senate abandoned efforts to pass legislation designed to restrict social media freedom more broadly in 2016, in response to public outcry and civil society criticism.[24] Looking ahead, it is more likely that powerful politicians and government agencies will seek to harness—and even manipulate—social media and new technology to their advantage, rather than undertake quixotic efforts to suppress them.

How will climate change impact Nigeria?

Nigeria is already grappling with many of the most devastating consequences of global climate change. Desertification, coastal inundation, and shifting weather patterns all seriously threaten the country. Looking ahead, high population growth, poor governance, and corruption—as well as man-made environmental threats like pollution and deforestation—will magnify the impact global climate change has on Nigeria.

Across Nigeria, human activity is exacerbating the effects of climate change. Though a product of climate change, the desertification of northern Nigeria is being accelerated by human activity such as overgrazing, slash-and-burn farming methods, and harvesting firewood. In some parts of the country, Sahara-like desert conditions are creeping southward by a few kilometers each year. In northeast Nigeria, successive droughts and intensive irrigation along its tributaries have caused Lake Chad to shrink dramatically since the mid-1960s.[25] The western, Nigeria-facing side of the lake is now choked with marshy islands and shallow channels. One fishing village that used to sit along the lake's edge is now twenty kilometers away from it.[26]

The disappearance through desiccation of northern Nigeria's once-productive farmlands and grazing areas has threatened the region's food security and triggered mass migration. This internal displacement of people in turn sparks land disputes. These struggles, especially those involving farmers and herdsmen, frequently turn deadly.[27] Since Nigeria derives more of its GDP from agriculture than from the oil and manufacturing sectors combined, desertification has also disproportionately hurt the economy.[28] Rural unemployment caused by desertification also contributed to the rise of Boko

Haram by providing the group with a large pool of idle youth from which to recruit.[29]

Like desertification, overgrazing is a decades-old phenomenon that worsens with each passing year. Nigeria's cattle population has risen in line with human population growth from an estimated 13.9 million in 1992 to 19.5 million in 2016.[30] In northeastern Nigeria, a telltale sign of overgrazing and worsening soil quality is the spread of mint and other weeds inedible by cattle.

Across many of the country's poorest and most desertification-prone states, more than 90 percent of households still depend on unsustainably harvested fuelwood, a major cause of deforestation.[31] Deforestation contributes to climate change in two ways: forests absorb carbon dioxide, acting as "sinks" for the greenhouse gas, and felled trees release carbon dioxide into the atmosphere.[32] Tree felling and unsustainable farming practices have also left communities vulnerable to severe gully erosion caused by heavy rains. Anambra State in southeastern Nigeria, where yawning gullies over one hundred feet deep routinely destroy homes and sever roads, is the epicenter of this environmental threat.[33]

Nigeria has one of the highest rates of deforestation in the world; between 2005 and 2015, parts of the country roughly the size of Switzerland were deforested.[34] Yet attempts to slow the destruction of rainforest in Cross River State, one of the world's most biodiverse ecosystems, have generated controversy. A logging moratorium drove up the price of timber, fanning black market trade by illegal loggers in cahoots with corrupt state officials.[35] And despite its own logging ban, the state government is pressing ahead with the construction of a 260-kilometer-long, six-lane superhighway straight through one of West Africa's remaining pristine rainforests.[36]

Coastal erosion is also accelerating as ongoing oil pollution and rising seas destroy the region's mangrove forests, an important ocean defense. Coastal inundation significantly threatens Nigeria's southern coast, including two

major cities: Lagos and Port Harcourt. The country's commercial capital, Lagos, which accounts for about 60 percent
of Nigeria's GDP, is vulnerably perched right at sea level. In
addition to submerging much of Lagos, a sea level rise of one
meter or more could cause the loss of 75 percent of Niger
Delta, the third largest wetland in the world and a major
carbon sink.[37]

For its part, the Nigerian government is not doing enough
to help arrest and eventually reverse the harmful effects of
global climate change. To do so, it must address the mismanagement and corruption that have undermined the country's
environmental, infrastructure, and transportation policies for
decades. Officials must incorporate measures to combat climate change and environmental degradation into the broader
spectrum of government policies, instead of fielding costly,
stand-alone, corruption-prone programs that have little long-
term impact.

On paper, Nigeria has many environmental remediation
programs, mostly because they have long been a conduit for
embezzlement and other forms of corruption. A recent audit
of the Ecological Fund—a voluminous federal fund for undertaking preventative and remedial environmental projects—
was the first since the fund was established in 1981.[38] It and
other investigations have revealed what many Nigerians already suspected: for decades politicians, civil servants, and
contractors have connived to embezzle billions of dollars in
environmental spending.[39]

Unless the Nigerian federal and state governments rein in
corruption and ramp up infrastructure spending exponentially, it is unlikely that Nigeria's international commitments
to cleaner and more efficient power generation, expanding the
use of mass transit, ending gas flaring, or reversing deforestation will be met by 2030. Bafflingly, the Nigerian government is
instead pursuing projects like the construction of Cross River's
rainforest-destroying superhighway and of coal-fired power
plants.[40]

To adapt to these threats and mitigate their impact, federal, state, and local governance needs to improve. Existing environmental laws need to be properly enforced and incentives provided to farmers, oil companies, and building contractors to embrace sustainable practices. Rather than reinstituting public fuel subsidies when oil prices rebound, the Nigerian government could, for example, subsidize solar home systems and clean cook stoves instead.

The good news for Nigeria is that the country's biggest environmental and economic problems share many of the same solutions. Increasing electrical power generation, for example, would spark socioeconomic development while also eliminating many Nigerians' need for noxious, inefficient diesel generators. Likewise, if it harnessed the roughly $5 billion worth of natural gas it flares each year, Nigeria could generate much-needed electricity or export it to neighboring countries, boosting its economy while also slashing carbon emissions.[41] Smarter urban planning and land management would also increase the profitability and environmental sustainability of Nigeria's sprawling cities as well as its forestry, livestock, and agricultural sectors.

Global efforts to mitigate climate change, especially the ongoing shift from fossil fuels toward renewables, may hurt the Nigerian economy in the short term by dampening demand for its main export: crude oil. Nigeria's long-term socioeconomic development, however, greatly depends on developed countries' efforts to slow, or even stop, man-made climate change. Its development potential also depends on the steps Nigerian officials and everyday citizens take to increase the country's resilience and reduce its vulnerability to climate change.

Will Nigeria's oil run out, and what happens if it does?

Nigeria currently is Africa's largest oil producer, but how much longer will it be so? Is Nigeria in danger of reaching its peak oil production, like neighboring Gabon and Cameroon?

Although forecasting future petroleum market trends is tricky, there is a growing consensus among petroleum market experts that global oil demand will peak before 2040.[42] Even though demand for crude oil is rising in developing countries, it is stagnating overall due to declining demand in Europe and North America as the share of wind and solar power increases and passenger cars become more fuel efficient.[43]

In light of these trends, Nigeria appears to be in no danger of exhausting its crude oil reserves. Oil-producing countries' output over time rarely follows a bell curve; production can decline and then grow again as new discoveries come online or as new technology extends the life span of existing fields.[44] That said, much of Nigeria's untapped reserves may be uneconomical to develop if global crude prices continue to stagnate, as they are located deep offshore. Shale oil deposits in central and northeast Nigeria will also be expensive to exploit and have yet to be explored. Even now, Nigeria is struggling to keep production costs down; among major oil producers, it ranks as the third most expensive place to produce a barrel of crude.[45]

If global demand for crude oil, Nigeria's main export, remains flat, the country's economy will suffer unless government and industry adapt accordingly. To start with, the government needs to update the petroleum sector's antiquated legal and regulatory framework. One proposed solution—the omnibus Petroleum Industry Bill (PIB)—was passed in 2017 but does not include many necessary reforms. Until they embrace international best practices, Nigeria's policymakers will struggle to make the country's petroleum sector a more attractive place to invest.

Another way Nigeria can help cushion the economic impact of peaking global crude demand is by facilitating investment in the country's budding petrochemical industry. Global petrochemical demand is set to remain high over the medium term, giving Nigeria an opportunity to diversify its petroleum-based exports.[46] To unlock this potential, however, the government must resolve a range of obstacles, such as foreign exchange controls, cumbersome regulations, natural-gas-to-power supply, and the ongoing mismanagement of the country's existing oil refineries.

When Nigeria someday does run out of oil—even if that happens next century—could there be a silver lining? For the last fifty years Nigeria has suffered from a "resource curse" in which its vast oil wealth has contaminated its political system, produced few socioeconomic gains, and fanned violence, especially in the oil-rich Niger Delta. Although Nigeria's astronomical oil wealth is not entirely to blame for these challenges, it fuels both the greed and grievances that perpetuate them.[47] With millions—sometimes billions—of portable petrodollars available for public officials to loot, any election that determines who controls government becomes, in the words of former president Obasanjo, a "do-or-die affair."[48]

As the share of GDP and, more importantly, government revenue derived from oil gradually declines, Nigeria's policymakers will need to redouble their efforts to diversify the country's economy and begin to rein in wasteful government spending. State governments will likewise need to cut red tape to become more business friendly so they can expand their tax base. If and when more Nigerians and domestic businesses begin to pay a greater share of their income in tax, their expectations of government and demand for public goods will increase. Over time, weaning the economy off oil may prompt Nigerians to see their officials more as stewards of their hard-earned tax money rather than as purveyors of near-limitless oil cash.

NOTES

Introduction

1. Nigerian—and African—official statistics are problematic. See Morten Jerven, *Poor Numbers: How We Are Misled by African Development Statistics and What to Do About It* (Ithaca, NY: Cornell University Press, 2013).

2. A regime is democratic if it holds credible elections in which the opposition has a reasonable chance of winning or taking office. The definition of democracy is from Robert A. Dahl, *Polyarchy: Participation and Opposition* (New Haven, CT: Yale University Press, 1971).

3. On the deep roots of corruption in Nigeria, see Stephen Ellis, *This Present Darkness* (Oxford: Oxford University Press, 2016). On US government efforts to assist Nigeria's struggle against corruption, see Matthew Page, *Improving U.S. Anticorruption Policy in Nigeria*, Council on Foreign Relations Corruption Brief (New York: Council on Foreign Relations, 2016); and John Campbell and Allen Grane, *How the Trump Administration Can Help Combat Kleptocracy in Africa*, Council on Foreign Relations Corruption Brief (New York: Council on Foreign Relations, 2017).

4. For an overview of Nigeria, see John Campbell, *Nigeria Dancing on the Brink*, updated ed. (Lanham, MD: Rowman & Littlefield, 2013).

5. The population figures relied on here are from the 2016 CIA *Factbook*. However, Nigeria's National Bureau of Statistics credibly cites a population of more than 200 million, rather than the *Factbook*'s 180 million. *The World Factbook (Nigeria)*

(Washington, DC: Central Intelligence Agency, 2016), https://
www.cia.gov/library/publications/the-world-factbook/.

6. Danzhen You, Lucia Hug, and David Anthony, *Generation
2030: Africa, Child Demographics in Africa*, UNICEF, 2014,
http://www.unicef.org/publications/files/UNICEF_Africa_
Generation_2030_en_11Aug.pdf.

7. Migration Policy Institute, *The Nigerian Diaspora in the United
States* (Washington, DC, Rockefeller Foundation–Aspen Institute
Diaspora Program, 2015).

8. Pidgin English is probably the most widely spoken language in
the country. By and large, non-Nigerian native English speakers
cannot understand it. One estimate is that perhaps half of the
population speaks enough English to communicate minimally
with a non-Nigerian English speaker. However, there is no
consensus about how many Nigerians speak "standard" English
as a first language.

9. On religion in Nigeria, see Pew Research Center, *Resources on
Islam and Christianity in Sub-Saharan Africa*, Pew Research Center,
2010, http://www.pewforum.org/2010/04/15/executive-
summary-islam-and-christianity-in-sub-saharan-africa/. The
report notes that 87 percent of Nigerians say religion is very
important in their lives. For comparison, in the United States
57 percent of those polled say religion is important in their lives.

10. Chinua Achebe, *The Trouble with Nigeria* (Johannesburg:
Heinemann, 1983), 2.

11. United Nations Department of Economic and Social Affairs/
Population Division, *World Population Prospects: The 2015 Revision,
Key Findings and Advance Tables*, Working Paper No. ESA/P/
WP.241 (New York: United Nations, 2015), https://esa.un.org/
unpd/wpp/publications/files/key_findings_wpp_2015.pdf.

12. National Population Commission (Nigeria), *Nigeria Demographic
and Health Survey 2013* (Abuja: National Population Commission,
2014), 68–69, https://dhsprogram.com/pubs/pdf/FR293/
FR293.pdf.

13. "Electricity in Nigeria: Powerless," *The Economist*, March
3, 2016, http://www.economist.com/news/middle-east-
and-africa/21693971-nigeria-has-about-much-electricity-
edinburgh-problem-powerless; Jonathan Nda-Isaiah,
"Nigeria Spent N2.7trn Power Generation in 16 Years,"
Leadership, September 9, 2015, http://web.archive.org/web/

20151224040815/http://leadership.ng/business/459605/
nigeria-spent-n2-7trn-power-generation-in-16-years.

14. UN Inter-agency Group for Child Mortality Estimation and
United Nations Population Division's World Population,
"Mortality Rate, Infant (per 1,000 Live Births)," The World Bank,
http://data.worldbank.org/indicator/SP.DYN.IMRT.IN?year_
high_desc=true.

15. Afrobarometer, "Opinions on Democracy and Accountability
Ahead of the 2015 Elections" (presentation, LinkedIn
Afrobarometer, March 23, 2015), http://www.slideshare.net/
Afrobarometer/nig-r6-presentation2democracy.

16. Femi Falana, "How Ex-Gov Modu Sheriff Sponsored Boko
Haram- Falana," *Premium Times*, September 4, 2014, http://
www.premiumtimesng.com/news/top-news/167724-how-ex-
gov-modu-sheriff-sponsored-boko-haram-falana.html.

17. "Nigeria Security Says Politicians Sponsor Islamists," *Reuters*,
November 21, 2011, http://af.reuters.com/article/nigeriaNews/
idAFL5E7ML2T320111121.

18. "Curbing Violence in Nigeria (II): The Boko Haram
Insurgency," International Crisis Group, April 3, 2014,
https://www.crisisgroup.org/africa/west-africa/nigeria/
curbing-violence-nigeria-ii-boko-haram-insurgency.

19. This report is based on a face-to-face Afrobarometer survey
in Nigeria among a representative sample of twenty-four
hundred adults aged eighteen and older. The survey has a
margin of error of approximately ±2 points. Akinremi Taofeeq
and Moses Olusola, "Afrobarometer Round 6 Survey, Nigeria
2015," Practical Sampling International, December 5, 2014–
January 19, 2015, http://afrobarometer.org/sites/default/files/
publications/Summary%20of%20results/nig_r6_sor_en.pdf.

20. Dave Joseph, "As Nigeria Battles Islamist Boko Haram, an
Imam and Pastor Spread Tolerance," *Christian Science Monitor*,
November 8, 2013, http://www.csmonitor.com/Commentary/
Common-Ground/2013/1108/As-Nigeria-battles-Islamist-Boko-
Haram-an-imam-and-pastor-spread-tolerance.

21. Taofeeq and Olusola, "Afrobarometer Round 6 Survey,
Nigeria 2015."

22. Stephanie Busari, "What Is behind Nigeria Fuel Protests?," *CNN*,
January 13, 2012, http://edition.cnn.com/2012/01/06/world/
africa/nigeria-fuel-protest-explained/.

23. Yaw Agyenim-Boateng, Richard Benson-Armer, and Bill Russo, "Winning in Africa's Consumer Market," *McKinsey and Company Consumer Packaged Goods* (blog), July 2015, http://www. mckinsey.com/industries/consumer-packaged-goods/our-insights/winning-in-africas-consumer-market.

24. Stephanie Busari, "Mark Zuckerberg's Visit Gives Nigerian Startups Much-needed Boost," *CNN*, September 1, 2016, http://edition.cnn.com/2016/08/31/africa/nigeria-zuckerberg-visit/.

Chapter 1: Historical Background

1. "This process was famously illustrated by Chinua Achebe in his novel *Things Fall Apart*"; Helen C. Metz, "The Emergence of Nigerian Nationality."

2. For a detailed study of the Nigerian Civil War, see John de St. Jorre, *The Brothers' War: Biafra and Nigeria* (Boston: Houghton Mifflin, 1972).

3. The quality of the election was so poor that former US president Jimmy Carter, serving as an election observer, left the country in disgust.

4. After Brazil abolished slavery in 1888, some Yoruba former slaves returned to Africa and settled in Lagos, a largely Yoruba city. Some of the houses in a Yoruba city neighborhood have a distinct Afro-Brazilian style reminiscent of Salvador do Bahia in northeast Brazil.

5. By 1902 slavery had been abolished in the Western Hemisphere, where the number of slaves, for example in Brazil and the American South, probably had been far larger than those trafficked by the Sultanate of Sokoto.

6. See Philip D. Curtin, *The Atlantic Slave Trade: A Census* (Madison: University of Wisconsin Press, 1972).

7. For the trans-Saharan slave trade, see Humphrey J. Fisher, *Slavery in the History of Muslim Black Africa* (New York: New York University Press, 2001).

8. Hillaire Belloc, *The Modern Traveller* (London: E. Arnold, 1898). The Gatling gun was a rapid-fire, spring-loaded predecessor to the machine gun.

9. John Robert Seely, *The Expansion of England,* (London: Macmillan & Co, 1883).

10. Lord Lugard set out his theory of indirect rule in *The Dual Mandate in British Tropical Africa*, 5th ed. (Abingdon, Oxon: F. Cass, 2005).

11. Chinua Achebe, *Once There Was a Country* (New York: Penguin Press, 2012).
12. The British divided Nigeria into three—later four—regions. As in Malaysia, the British saw a federation as a means of unifying people of disparate ethnicities and religions. In Nigeria, regional governments had some autonomy, though not as much as American states do.
13. Ojukwu was a colonel in the Nigerian federal army. Enugu, the capital of the eastern region, was the capital of Biafra until it was occupied by federal troops.
14. On the Biafra War, see de St. Jorre, *The Brothers' War: Biafra and Nigeria.*
15. Gowon went into exile in the United Kingdom, pursuing a PhD in political science from the University of Warwick. Implicated in the failed Dimka coup in 1975, Gowon was stripped of his pension. However, civilian president Shehu Shagari eventually pardoned him and former Biafran head of state Ojukwu in 1982. Gowon returned to Nigeria in 1983. Then military chief of state Ibrahim Babangida finally restored his military rank in 1987.
16. This is now part of the national myth. However, there are whispers that Obasanjo's handover was not voluntary but rather was forced by his fellow military rivals and colleagues.
17. In fact, the Nigerian constitution is only reminiscent of that of the United States. For example, the Nigerian constitution is 47,200 words long, while the US Constitution (including signatures and amendments) is only 7,400.
18. Champagne consumption was illegal, a measure designed to conserve foreign exchange. Under the Second Republic, "big men" were notorious for drinking champagne at all hours, thereby demonstrating that they were above the law.
19. Its name varied over time. It was usually made up of representatives of the army, navy, and air force at the colonel or brigadier general level, with the army predominating.
20. Why the military objected to Abiola has never been adequately explained.
21. The myth on the street is that Abacha was poisoned by two Indian prostitutes with whom he was cavorting.
22. In almost every coup soldiers or police were killed, but there was never a mass slaughter.

23. Flight Lieutenant Jerry Rawlings staged a successful military coup in Ghana in 1981. The legend is that he destroyed much of the traditional establishment and then rebuilt an uncorrupt, democratic Ghana from the ground up. In fact, he murdered only a handful of leading political figures, but his victims did include three former heads of state.

24. Prebendalism is a system in which individuals access government revenue to advance themselves and their families, religions, and ethnic groups. The seminal work on prebendalism is Richard Joseph, *Democracy and Prebendal Politics in Nigeria* (Cambridge, UK: Cambridge University Press, 1982).

25. Abubakar Tafawa Balewa, the first prime minister of an independent Nigeria, might also be included. However, his influence was limited by his murder in the 1966 coup. He was only forty-four years old at his death. Ahmadu Bello was also murdered in the 1966 coup.

26. On Ahmadu Bello, see John N. Paden, *Ahmadu Bello, Sardauna of Sokoto* (Zaria: Hudahuda Publishing Co., 1986). On Nnandi Azikiwe, see K. A. B. Jones-Quartey, *A Life of Azikiwe* (Baltimore, MD: Penguin, 1965). On Obafemi Awolowo, see his autobiography, *Awo: The Autobiography of Chief Obafemi Awolowo* (Cambridge, UK: Cambridge University Press, 1960). On Biafran chief of state Ojukwu, see Frederick Forsyth, *Emeka* (Ibadan, Nigeria: Spectrum Books, 1992). On Nigeria's first prime minister, Tafawa Balewa, see Trevor Clark, *A Right Honourable Gentleman: Abubakar from the Black Rock, a Narrative Chronicle of the Life and Times of Nigeria's Alhaji Sir Abubakar Tafawa Balewa* (London: Edward Arnold, 1991).

27. Successive civilian governments have struggled to repatriate the funds Abacha and his associates looted, achieving only limited success.

Chapter 2: The Economics of Oil

1. For more information see Morton Jerven, *Poor Numbers: How We Are Misled by African Development Statistics and What to Do About It* (Ithaca, NY: Cornell University Press, 2013).

2. Mayowa Tijani, "Garri N10k, Rice N17k, Kerosene N450 . . . Nigerians Groan as Cost of Living Soars," *The Cable*, January 18, 2017, https://www.thecable.ng/how-govt-policies-lower-living-standards-push-millions-of-nigerians-into-poverty.

3. Everest Amaefule, "Nigeria Hasn't Attracted Any Major Mining Operator—FG," *The Punch*, January 4, 2017, http://punchng. com/nigeria-hasnt-attracted-major-mining-operator-fg/.

4. Peter Lewis, *Growing Apart: Oil, Politics, and Economic Change in Indonesia and Nigeria* (Ann Arbor: University of Michigan Press, 2007), 169.

5. Festus Akanbi, "Understanding CBN's Anchor Borrowers' Programme," *This Day*, November 21, 2015, http://allafrica. com/stories/201511231656.html.

6. Dayo Aiyetan and Habeeb Pindiga, "Investigation: Fertiliser Fraud Thrives Despite Government's Claim Sector Is Sanitized," *Premium Times*, October 5, 2013, http://www.premiumtimesng. com/news/146073-investigation-fertiliser-fraud-thrives-despite-governments-claim-sector-is-sanitized.html.

7. World Bank, *Ease of Doing Business Index 2017: Nigeria*, http:// www.doingbusiness.org/data/exploreeconomies/nigeria.

8. *Nigeria's Oil and Gas Industry Brief* (Lagos, Nigeria: KPMG Nigeria, June 2014), 5.

9. Matthew T. Page, "Nigeria's Reform of Its State Oil Company Will Be Cosmetic Without Cutting Corrupt Ties," *Quartz Africa*, March 11, 2016, https://qz.com/636391/nigerias-reform-of-its-state-oil-company-will-be-cosmetic-without-cutting-corrupt-ties/.

10. "FAAC Disburses N386bn to FG, States, LGs in November 2016," *Vanguard*, December 15, 2016, http://www.vanguardngr.com/ 2016/12/faac-disburses-n386bn-fg-states-lgs-november-2016/.

11. Nigeria's current oil-producing states are Bayelsa, Rivers, Delta, Akwa Ibom, Edo, Ondo, Lagos, Abia, and Imo. Lagos only joined the list in 2016 after the Aje oilfield began commercial production.

12. Between 1999 and 2012, Cross River was an oil-producing state. Following a 2012 court decision mandating it cede its few oil wells to neighboring Akwa Ibom State, it no longer produced oil.

13. National Bureau of Statistics, *Harmonized Nigeria Living Standard Survey, 2010* (Abuja, Nigeria: National Bureau of Statistics, 2012), 11, http://www.nigerianstat.gov.ng/pdfuploads/Nigeria%20 Poverty%20Profile%202010.pdf.

14. United Nations Development Program Country Office in Nigeria, *National Human Development Report, 2015: Human Security and Human Development in Nigeria* (distributed by the

United Nations Development Program, 2015), http://hdr.undp. org/sites/default/files/2016_national_human_development_ report_for_nigeria.pdf.

15. John Elnathan, "How to Identify a Middle Class Nigerian," *Elnathan's Dark Corner*, June 6, 2015, http://elnathanjohn.blogspot. co.uk/2015/06/how-to-identify-middle-class-nigerian.html.

16. Named after the Italian statistician who developed it, Corrado Gini, this method measures the distribution of wealth or economic inequality in a country. Inequality on the Gini scale is measured between 0 (complete equality) and 1 (complete inequality). The higher a country's Gini coefficient, the greater its income divide between rich and poor.

17. World Bank, *World Development Indicators, 2013* (Washington, DC: World Bank, 2013, distributed by United Nations Development Program, Human Development Reports), http:// hdr.undp.org/en/content/income-gini-coefficient.

18. National Bureau of Statistics, *Harmonized Nigeria Living Standard Survey*, 23.

19. Gabriel Omoh, "Capital Flight: Economy Hard Hit by $22.1bn Outflow in 5 Weeks," *Vanguard*, February 23, 2015, http://www. vanguardngr.com/2015/02/capital-flight-economy-hard-hit-by-22-1bn-outflow-in-5-weeks/.

20. Dev Kar and Joseph Spanjers, "Illicit Financial Flows from Developing Countries: 2004–2013," *Global Financial Integrity*, December 8, 2015, http://www.gfintegrity.org/report/illicit-financial-flows-from-developing-countries-2004-2013/.

21. Sanusi Lamido Sanusi, "Growth Prospects for the Nigerian Economy" (convocation lecture, delivered at Igbinedion University, Edo State, Nigeria, November 26, 2010).

22. Klaus Schwab, *The Global Competitiveness Report 2016–2017* (Geneva: World Economic Forum, 2016), https://www.weforum. org/reports/the-global-competitiveness-report-2016-2017-1.

23. Calculated using the Ministry of Budget and National Planning's 2017 Budget Proposal.

24. BudgIT, *The State of the States: 2015* (Lagos: BudgIT, 2015), 59.

25. African Development Bank, Organisation for Economic Co-operation and Development, United Nations Development Programme, *Africa Economic Outlook 2015: Nigeria Country Note* (Paris, France: African Development Bank, 2015), 8.

26. Based on Lloyd's List Intelligence APEX tanker data. US Energy Information Administration, *Country Analysis Brief: Nigeria* (Washington, DC: US Energy Information Administration, 2016), https://www.eia.gov/beta/international/analysis.cfm?iso=NGA.

27. Ibid. Matthew Page, "(Re)Emerging Threats to Nigeria's Petroleum Sector: Militancy, Mismanagement, and Low Oil Prices," Columbia University Center for Energy Policy, December 1, 2016, http://energypolicy.columbia.edu/publications/commentary/reemerging-threats-nigerias-petroleum-sector-militancy-mismanagement-low-oil-prices.

28. Daniel Jordan Smith, *A Culture of Corruption: Everyday Deception and Popular Discontent in Nigeria* (Princeton, NJ: Princeton University Press, 2010), 20.

29. International Cocoa Organization (ICCO), "Cocoa Year 2015/16," *ICCO Quarterly Bulletin of Cocoa Statistics* 42, no. 3 (August 31, 2016), https://www.icco.org/about us/international-cocoa-agreements/doc_download/240-production-latest-figures-from-the-quarterly-bulletin-of-cocoa-statistics.html.

30. The Observatory of Economic Complexity, *Where Does Nigeria Export Cocoa To?*, 2014, http://atlas.media.mit.edu/en/visualize/tree_map/hs92/export/nga/show/1801/2014/.

31. Ibid.

32. Food and Agriculture Organization of the United Nations (FAO), *2014 Global Crop Statistics for Sesame Seed*, http://www.fao.org/faostat/en/#data.

33. Olushola Bello, "Reviving Nigeria's Ailing Textile Industry for Job Creation," *Leadership*, January 24, 2016, http://leadership.ng/news/494633/reviving-nigerias-ailing-textile-industry-job-creation.

34. Yepoka Yeebo, "African Traders Flocked to Guangzhou for the Cheap Goods But Are Staying to Run Manufacturing Operations," *Quartz Africa*, May 13, 2013, https://qz.com/81642/african-traders-flocked-to-guangzhou-for-the cheap-goods-but-are-staying-to-run-manufacturing-operations/.

35. Uche Nzeka and Joshua Taylor, "Nigeria: Grain and Feed Update" (Global Agricultural Information Network, 2016; distributed by US Foreign Agricultural Service), https://gain.fas.usda.gov/Recent%20GAIN%20Publications/Grain%20and%20Feed%20Update_Lagos_Nigeria_11-9-2016.pdf.

36. Kate Douglas, "Domino's Pizza Aiming to Be the Big Cheese in Nigeria," *How We Made It in Africa*, January 20, 2014, http://www.howwemadeitinafrica.com/dominos-pizza-aiming-to-be-the-big-cheese-in-nigeria/.

37. "Murray-Bruce Supports Local Manufacturers, Buys Innoson Cars," *The Punch*, February 15, 2016, http://punchng.com/murray-bruce-buys-innoson-cars-in-support-of-local-manufacturers/.

38. Henry Umoru, "Saraki Lauds Nigerian Army for Buying Aba Made Shoes," *Vanguard*, October 30, 2016, http://www.vanguardngr.com/2016/10/saraki-lauds-nigerian-army-for-buying-aba-made-shoes/.

39. Lee Yuan Kew, *From Third World to First: The Singapore Story 1965–2000* (New York: HarperCollins, 2000), 393; also quoted in Greg Mills, *Why States Recover: Changing Walking Societies into Winning Nations, from Afghanistan to Zimbabwe* (Oxford: Oxford University Press, 2015), 107.

40. Olu Fasan, "Nigeria's Import Restrictions: A Bad Policy That Harms Trade Relations," *Africa at LSE [London School of Economics]* (blog), August 17, 2015, http://blogs.lse.ac.uk/africaatlse/2015/08/17/nigerias-import-restrictions-a-bad-policy-that-harms-trade-relations/.

41. The Economist Group Limited, "Building on Concrete Foundations," *The Economist*, April 12, 2014, http://www.economist.com/news/business/21600688-mix-natural-advantages-and-protectionism-has-made-dangote-group-nigerias-biggest-firm-now.

Chapter 3: Religion

1. A small minority of ethnic Igbos in southeastern Nigeria claim to be Jewish and argue that they have the right to immigrate to Israel under the Law of Return. However, their claim is not recognized by the Jewish religious authorities in Jerusalem, and the Israeli government does not permit their immigration on that basis.

2. Forty-six percent of the population was raised Christian and is currently Christian. Fifty-two percent was raised Muslim and is currently Muslim. Pew Research Center Forum on Religion and Public Life, *Tolerance and Tension: Islam and Christianity in Sub-Saharan Africa* (Washington, DC: Pew Research Center, 2010, 19).

3. Carlyle Murphy, "Q & A: The Muslim-Christian Education Gap in sub-Saharan Africa," Pew Research Center, December 14, 2016, http://www.pewresearch.org/fact-tank/2016/12/14/qa-the-muslim-christian-education-gap-in-sub-saharan-africa/.

4. Pew Research Center, *Resources on Islam and Christianity in Sub-Saharan Africa* (Pew Research Center, 2010), http://assets.pewresearch.org/wp-content/uploads/sites/11/2010/04/sub-saharan-africa-full-report.pdf.

5. Nigerian Television Authority, June 16, 2016; *Premium Times*, March 31, 2017.

6. Pew Research Center, "The World's Muslims: Religion, Politics and Society," Pew Research Center, April 30, 2013, http://www.pewforum.org/2013/04/30/the-worlds-muslims-religion-politics-society-overview/.

7. Pew Research Center, "Spirit and Power—A 10-Country Survey of Pentecostals," Pew Research Center, December 5, 2006, http://www.pewforum.org/2006/10/05/spirit-and-power/.

Chapter 4: Politics: Nigeria's Great Game

1. Richard Joseph, *Democracy and Prebendal Politics in Nigeria: The Rise and Fall of the Second Republic* (Ibadan, Nigeria: Spectrum Books, 1987).

2. "Nigeria - Executive Summary." Export.gov. July 13, 2016. Accessed December 06, 2017. https://www.export.gov/apex/article2?id=Nigeria-Executive-Summary

3. Naziru Mikailu, "Nigeria's Cabinet: Seven People to Watch in Buhari's Team," *BBC News*, November 11, 2015, http://www.bbc.co.uk/news/world-africa-34538718.

4. To date, no Nigerian state has elected a female governor. Virginia Etiaba served as acting governor of Anambra State from November 2006 to February 2007 before the courts reinstated impeached governor Peter Obi. In 2015 Aisha Jummai Al-Hassan narrowly lost the Taraba State gubernatorial election, almost making history. See Chapter 4 for more on the role of women in Nigerian politics.

5. Jude Okafor, "Local Government Financial Autonomy in Nigeria: The State Joint Local Government Account," *Commonwealth Journal of Local Governance* (July 2010): 128.

6. Human Rights Watch, *Arbitrary Killings by Security Forces: Submission to the Investigative Bodies on the November*

28–29, 2008 *Violence in Jos, Plateau State, Nigeria* (Washington, DC: Human Rights Watch, 2009), 9.

7. Veteran state politician, Gombe State, interview by Matthew Page, September 21, 2016.

8. For more information, see Adebowale Olorunmola, *The Cost of Politics in Nigeria*, The Westminster Foundation for Democracy, http://www.wfd.org/wp-content/uploads/2016/07/Nigeria-Cost-of-Politics.pdf.

9. Daniel Jordan Smith, *A Culture of Corruption: Everyday Deception and Popular Discontent in Nigeria* (Princeton, NJ: Princeton University Press, 2010), 224–225.

10. Wale Odunsi, "EFCC Will Recruit 750 Staff in 2016—Magu," *Daily Post*, February 8, 2016, http://dailypost.ng/2016/02/08/efcc-will-recruit-750-staff-in-2016-magu/.

11. Sebastine Ebhuomhan, "Corruption: EFCC 'Secured about 1,500 Convictions in 14 Years'—Official," *Premium Times*, February 16, 2017, http://www.premiumtimesng.com/news/more-news/223742-corruption-efcc-secured-1-500-convictions-2016-official.html.

12. "TCN Wants EFCC Insulated from Political Control," *The Guardian* (Nigeria), May 14, 2015, http://guardian.ng/news/tcn-wants-efcc-insulated-from-political-control/.

13. Human Rights Watch, *Corruption on Trial? The Record of Nigeria's Economic and Financial Crimes Commission* (New York: Human Rights Watch, 2011), 46, https://www.hrw.org/sites/default/files/reports/nigeria0811WebToPost.pdf.

14. Kunle Olasanmi, "AGF Stops CCB Chairman from Making Public, Assets Declaration Form," *Leadership*, January 20, 2017, http://leadership.ng/news/cover-stories/567901/agf-stops-ccb-chairman-from-making-public-assets-declaration-form.

15. Constitution of the Federal Republic of Nigeria (1999), Third Schedule, Part I, §3 (c), http://www.justice.gov.ng/images/Downloads/Constitution/Nigerian%20Constitution.pdf.

16. Evelyn Okakwu, "Exclusive: Untold Story of SSS Raids on Judges' Homes in Abuja, Five States," *Premium Times*, October 8, 2016, http://www.premiumtimesng.com/news/headlines/212351-exclusive-untold-story-sss-raids-judges-homes-abuja-five-states.html.

17. Matthew Page, *Improving U.S. Corruption Policy in Nigeria* (Washington, DC: Council on Foreign Relations, 2016), http://

www.cfr.org/nigeria/improving-us-anticorruption-policy-nigeria/p38123.

18. Dimeji Kayode-Adedeji, "PDP Died After My Exit—Obasanjo," *Premium Times*, March 3, 2017, http://www.premiumtimesng.com/news/headlines/225157-pdp-died-exit-obasanjo.html.

19. A faction of the southeast-oriented APGA also joined the APC at the time.

20. Michael Egbejumi-David, "How to Be a Local Government Chairman," *Sahara Reporters*, February 23, 2011, http://saharareporters.com/2011/02/23/how-be-local-government-chairman.

21. National chairman of an opposition political party, interview by Matthew Page, March 2, 2017.

22. Gombe State legislative candidate, interview by Matthew Page, September 21, 2016.

23. "How Governors Rig Elections, by Donald Duke," *The Guardian* (Nigeria), distributed by Sahara Reporters, July18, 2010, http://saharareporters.com/2010/07/18/must-read-how-governors-rig-elections-donald-duke-guardian.

24. Pat Ama Tokunbo Williams, "Women and the Dilemma of Politics in Nigeria," in *Dilemmas of Democracy in Nigeria*, ed. Paul A. Beckett and Crawford Young (Rochester: University of Rochester, 1997), 222–223.

25. Former state legislator, interview by Matthew Page, September 19, 2016.

26. Interparliamentary Union, "Women in National Parliaments: Situation as of 1st January 2017," http://www.ipu.org/wmn-e/classif.htm.

27. Kanayo Jubal Onukogu, "Margaret Ekpo—Fierce Defender of Women's Rights," *Leadership*, December 13, 2013, http://allafrica.com/stories/201312130088.html.

28. Onyeka Onwenu, "Interview with Chief Mrs Margaret Ekpo," *Chinua Achebe Foundation*, July 10, 2005, http://www.nigerialinks.com/Articles/CAchebe/2005/07/foundation-interviews-9-chief-mrs.html.

29. Awike Nwodo, "Patience Jonathan Urges Women to Vote for PDP," Naij.com, January 9, 2015, https://politics.naij.com/358202-patience-jonathan-urges-women-to-vote-for-pdp.html; Solomon Ayado, "Jonathan'll Grant 45%

Affirmative Action to Women—Dame Patience," *Leadership*, February 28, 2015, http://leadership.ng/news/414369/ jonathanll-grant-45-affirmative-action-to-women-dame-patience.

Chapter 5: Nigeria's Security Challenges

1. Alex Thurston, "'The Disease Is Unbelief': Boko Haram's Religious and Political Worldview," in *The Brookings Project on U.S. Relations with the Islamic World* (Washington, DC: Brookings Institution, 2016), 22:5.
2. John Campbell, *Nigeria Security Tracker*, March 23, 2017, distributed by Africa Program, Council on Foreign Relations, http://www.cfr.org/nigeria/nigeria-security-tracker/p29483.
3. Ibid.
4. Anonymous, "The Popular Discourses of Salafi Radicalism and Salafi Counter-radicalism in Nigeria: A Case Study of Boko Haram," *Journal of Religion in Africa* 42 (2012): 127.
5. Ibid., 122.
6. International Crisis Group, *Curbing Violence in Nigeria (II): The Boko Haram Insurgency* (Washington, DC: International Crisis Group, 2014), 12.
7. Andrew Walker, *What Is Boko Haram?* (Washington, DC: United States Institute of Peace, 2012), 4.
8. Walter E. A. Van Beek, "Intensive Slave Raiding in the Colonial Interstice: Hamman Yaji and the Mandara Mountains (North Cameroon and North-Eastern Nigeria)," *Journal of African History* 53 (2012): 303.
9. World Food Program, "Nigeria Situation Report #9, 1–15 March 2017," Relief Web, March 15, 2017, http://reliefweb.int/report/ nigeria/wfp-nigeria-situation-report-9-1-15-march-2017.
10. Matthew T. Page and A. Carl LeVan, "Donors Dither as Bureaucrats Exploit Nigeria's Humanitarian Crisis," AllAfrica. com, October 16, 2016, http://allafrica.com/stories/ 201610160399.html; Donald G. McNeil Jr., "Malnutrition Wiping Out Children in Northern Nigeria, Aid Workers Say," *New York Times*, January 23, 2017, https://www.nytimes.com/2017/01/ 23/health/malnutrition-nigeria-children.html.
11. Ukoha Ukiwo, "From 'Pirates' to 'Militants': A Historical Perspective on Anti-State and Anti-Oil Company Mobilization among the Ijaw of Warri, Western Niger Delta," *African Affairs* 106 (2007): 592–593.

12. *Report of the Commission Appointed to Enquire into the Fears of Minorities and the Means of Allaying Them—the "Willink" Commission* (London: Colonial Office, 1958), 95, http://eie.ng/wp-content/uploads/2014/03/TheWillinkCommissionReport_conc_recom_lt.pdf.

13. "Crackdown in the Niger Delta," *Human Rights Watch* 11 (1999): A, https://www.hrw.org/reports/1999/nigeria2/index.htm.

14. Elias Courson, *Movement for the Emancipation of the Niger Delta (MEND) Political Marginalization, Repression and Petro-insurgency in the Niger Delta* (Uppsala: Nordiska Afrikainstitutet, 2009), 18.

15. *Nigeria Watch: Sixth Report on Violence in Nigeria (2016)* (Abuja: Nigeria Stability and Reconciliation Programme, 2017), 16, http://www.nigeriawatch.org/media/html/NGA-Watch-Report16V7.pdf.

16. For more information, see Ifeanyi Onwuzuruigbo, "Horizontal Inequalities and Communal Conflicts: The Case of Aguleri and Umuleri Communities of South-Eastern Nigeria," *Africa* 81 (2011): 567–587.

17. *The Economic Costs of Conflict and the Benefits of Peace: Effects of Farmer-Pastoralist Conflict in Nigeria's Middle Belt on State, Sector, and National Economies* (Washington, DC: MercyCorps, 2015), https://www.mercycorps.org/sites/default/files/Mercy%20Corps%20Nigeria%20State%20Costs%20of%20Conflict%20Policy%20Brief%20July%202015.pdf.

18. For more on the motivations of the January 1966 coup leaders, see Adewale Ademoyega, *Why We Struck: The Story of the First Nigerian Coup* (Ibadan: Evans Brothers [Nigeria Publishers] Ltd., 2015).

19. Jimi Peters, *The Nigerian Military and the State* (London: I. B. Tauris, 1997), 118.

20. Ibid., 145.

21. "Corruption Flourished in Abacha's Regime," *Washington Post*, June 9, 1998, http://www.washingtonpost.com/wp-srv/inatl/longterm/nigeria/stories/corrupt060998.htm.

22. "U.S. to Help Nigeria Revamp Its Armed Forces," *Washington Post*, April 29, 2000, https://www.washingtonpost.com/archive/politics/2000/04/29/us-to-help-nigeria-revamp-its-armed-forces/eab2413a-3264-4812-8375-ca1c54fa6d29/.

23. Robert S. Smith, *Kingdoms of the Yoruba* (London: James Curry Ltd., 1988), 166.

24. Matthew T. Page, "Improving US Corruption Policy in Nigeria," Council on Foreign Relations, 2016, http://www.cfr.org/nigeria/improving-us-anticorruption-policy-nigeria/p38123.

25. Transparency International, *Government Defence Anti-Corruption Index 2015: Nigeria* (London: Transparency International, 2015), https://government.defenceindex.org/countries/nigeria/.

26. Ernest Ogbozor, *Understanding the Informal Security Sector in Nigeria* (Washington, DC: United States Institute of Peace, 2016), http://www.usip.org/publications/2016/09/15/understanding-the-informal-security-sector-in-nigeria.

27. Thirty-six states plus the Federal Capital Territory (FCT).

28. Budget Office of the Federation, Ministry of Budget and National Planning, *2017 Federal Government of Nigeria Budget Proposal* (Lagos: Federal Government of Nigeria, 2016).

29. Yomi Kazeem, "Up to Three-Quarters of Nigeria's Prison Population Is Serving Time Without Being Sentenced," *Quartz Africa*, January 24, 2017, https://qz.com/892498/up-to-three-quarters-of-nigerias-prison-population-is-serving-time-without-being-sentenced/.

30. *Pretrial Detention and Torture: Why Pretrial Detainees Face the Greatest Risk* (New York: Open Society Foundations, 2011), 18, https://www.opensocietyfoundations.org/sites/default/files/pretrial-detention-and-torture-06222011.pdf.

31. "Policing Communal Conflicts: The State, Parallel Security Providers, and Communities," Nigeria Research Network, University of Oxford, March 2013, http://www3.qeh.ox.ac.uk/pdf/nrn/nrn-pb04.pdf.

32. Kialee Nyiayaana, "Arming Community Vigilantes in the Niger Delta: Implications for Peacebuilding," in *African Frontiers: Insurgency, Governance and Peacebuilding in Postcolonial States*, ed. John Idriss Lahai and Tanya Lyons (London: Routledge, 2015), 135–136.

33. International Crisis Group, *Boko Haram on the Back Foot?* (Brussels: International Crisis Group, 2016), 7.

Chapter 6: Nigeria and the World

1. "Overseas Chinese Businesses Sprout up in Nigeria," *Skyline Monthly*, June 2006.

2. Adams Bodono, *Africans in China* (Amherst, NY: Cambria Press, 2012).

3. Ian Taylor, "Sino-Nigerian Relations," *China Brief—Jamestown Foundation 7*, no. 11 (May 2007), https://jamestown.org/program/sino-nigerian-relations-ftzs-textiles-and-oil-2/.

4. Akinkunmi Akingbade, "Reviewing China-Nigeria Trade Relations," *Ventures Africa*, September 29, 2016, http://venturesafrica.com/reviewing-china-nigeria-trade-relations/.

5. For the 2016 human rights report on Nigeria, see Bureau of Democracy, Human Rights and Labor, *Country Reports on Human Rights Practices for 2016 (Nigeria)*, at US Department of State, https://www.state.gov/j/drl/rls/hrrpt/humanrightsreport/#wrapper.

6. Pew Research Center, "The Global Divide on Homosexuality," Pew Research Center, June 4, 2013, 3 http://www.pewglobal.org/2013/06/04/the-global-divide-on-homosexuality/

7. "Nigeria: The Children—Education," United Nations International Children's Emergency Fund, https://www.unicef.org/nigeria/children_1937.html.

8. Committee to Protect Journalists, *Attacks on the Press* (Hoboken, NJ: John Wiley Inc., 2013), 40–41.

9. "Nigerians Abroad: Secret Weapon," *The Economist*, June 18, 2015, http://www.economist.com/news/special-report/21654360-nigerias-diaspora-source-money-markets-skills-and-ideas-secret-weapon

10. Migration Policy Institute, *The Nigerian Diaspora in the United States*, June 2015 revised. Migration Policy Institute, www.migrationpolicy.org/sites/default/files/publications/RAD-Nigeria.pdf.

11. Ibid.

12. John Campbell, "Africa's Brain Drain: Nigerian Medical Doctors," Council on Foreign Relations, October 29, 2013, https://www.cfr.org/blog-post/africas-brain-drain-nigerian-medical-doctors.

13. On Nollywood, see Norimitsu Onishi, "How *The Times* Named Nollywood," *New York Times*, February 11, 2016, https://www.nytimes.com/2016/02/11/insider/how-the-times-named-nollywood.html?_r=0; and "Nigeria's Booming Film Industry Redefines African Life," *New York Times*, February 18, 2016, https://www.nytimes.com/2016/02/19/world/africa/

with-a-boom-before-the-cameras-nigeria-redefines-african-life.
html.

Chapter 7: Nigeria of the Future

1. United Nations Population Division, *World Urbanization Prospects* (New York: United Nations, 2014).
2. Adzandeh Emmanuel Ayila, Fabiyi O. Oluseyi, and Bello Yakasai Anas, "Statistical Analysis of Urban Growth in Kano Metropolis, Nigeria," *International Journal of Environmental Monitoring and Analysis* 2 (2014): 55.
3. "Police Displace Thousands in Nigeria's Otodo-Gbame Slum," Al-Jazeera, March 18, 2017, http://www.aljazeera.com/news/2017/03/police-displace-thousands-nigeria-otodo-gbame-slum-170318190442226.html.
4. Côme Salvaire and Charlie Mitchell, "'It's Like a Civil War': In Lagos, Land Clearances Can Be Fatal," *CityMetric*, December 1, 2016, http://www.citymetric.com/fabric/it-s-civil-war-lagos-land-clearances-can-be-fatal-2627.
5. "The Port Harcourt Waterfront: Confronting the Curse of an Oil City," *Vanguard*, December 9, 2009, http://www.vanguardngr.com/2009/12/the-port-harcourt-waterfront-confronting-the-curse-of-an-oil-city/.
6. A. Carl LeVan and Josiah Olubowale, "'I Am Here Until Development Comes': Displacement, Demolitions, and Property Rights in Urbanizing Nigeria," *African Affairs* 113 (2014): 387.
7. Laurent Fourchard, "Bureaucrats and Indigenes: Producing and Bypassing Certificates of Origin in Nigeria," *Africa: The Journal of the International African Institute* 85 (2015): 43–44.
8. Okezie A. Odoemene and Akachi Odoemene, "Perspectives on Migration, Urbanisation and Development in Two 'New' African Cities: Trends, Dynamics and Post-Colonial Implications," 18, http://paa2012.princeton.edu/papers/120396.
9. "Off-grid Solar Power: Africa Unplugged," *The Economist*, October 29, 2016, http://www.economist.com/news/middle-east-and-africa/21709297-small-scale-solar-power-surging-ahead-africa-unplugged.
10. "Lagos: The Megacity Battling for Water," CNN, May 23, 2017, http://www.cnn.com/2017/05/23/africa/gallery/lagos-water-system/.
11. Scheduled to be completed in late 2016, the long-awaited twenty-seven-kilometer-long Blue Line light railway system

remains under construction. Since 2008 Lagos has operated a bus rapid transit system (BRT) along one twenty-two-kilometer north–south route.

12. Aida Aki, "Nigerians Take to Mobile for Better Media Content," in *How We Made It in Africa*, December 1, 2015, https://www.howwemadeitinafrica.com/nigerians- take-to-mobile-for-better-media-content.

13. Simon Kemp, *We Are Social*, January 27, 2016, https://wearesocial.com/uk/special-reports/digital-in-2016.

14. *Contemporary Media Use in Nigeria*, Broadcasting Board of Governors (United States), 2014, https://www.bbg.gov/wp-content/media/2014/05/Nigeria-research-brief.pdf.

15. Ibid.

16. Kemp, *We Are Social*, 2016.

17. Stephanie Busari, "Mark Zuckerberg's Visit Gives Nigerian Startups Much-Needed Boost," CNN, September 1, 2016, http://edition.cnn.com/2016/08/31/africa/nigeria-zuckerberg-visit/.

18. Christine Mungai, "How Africa Tweets: 10 Very Surprising Trends and Insights, Including That Japanese and Korean Are 'African,'" *Mail and Guardian Africa*, April 7, 2016, http://mgafrica.com/article/2016-04-07-how-africa-tweets-surprising- trends-and-insights.

19. Jerri Eddings, "The Power of Social Media in the Nigerian Election," International Center for Journalists, April 20, 2015, https://www.icfj.org/blogs/power-social-media-nigerian-election.

20. Audu Liberty Oseni, "Social Media Revolutionizes Nigerian Election," *Pambazuka News*, April 8, 2015, http://allafrica.com/stories/201504141451.html.

21. Alexa.com, http://www.alexa.com/topsites/countries/NG.

22. Samuel Ogundipe, "Again, Police Arrest Audu Maikori, Chocolate City Boss," *Premium Times*, March 10, 2017, http://www.premiumtimesng.com/news/top-news/225795-police-arrest-audu-maikori-chocolate-city-boss-2.html.

23. Cordelia Hebblethwaite, "#BBCtrending: The Man Who 'Disappeared' in Nigeria—#FreeCiaxon," *BBC Trending* (blog), April 11, 2014, http://www.bbc.co.uk/news/blogs-trending-26979508.

24. Hassan Adebayo, "Senate Bows to Public Pressure, Withdraws Anti-Social Media Bill," *Premium Times*, May 17, 2016, http://

www.premiumtimesng.com/news/top-news/203548-breaking-
senate-bows-public-pressure-withdraws-anti-social-media-bill.
html.

25. United States Geological Survey, "Earthshots: Satellite Images
    of Environmental Change: Lake Chad, West Africa," accessed
    January 11, 2017, https://earthshots.usgs.gov/earthshots/
    Lake-Chad-West-Africa.

26. Ahmed Salkida, "Africa's Vanishing Lake Chad," *Africa Renewal*,
    April 2012, http://www.un.org/africarenewal/magazine/april-
    2012/africa%E2%80%99s-vanishing-lake-chad.

27. Aaron Sayne, *Rethinking Nigeria's Indigene-Settler Conflicts*
    (Washington, DC: United States Institute of Peace, 1992).

28. National Bureau of Statistics, Nigeria, "Nigerian Gross
    Domestic Product Report Q3 2016," November 21, 2016, http://
    nigerianstat.gov.ng/report/469.

29. Theresa Krinninger, "Lake Chad: Climate Chad Fosters
    Terrorism," *Deutsche Welle*, December 7, 2015, http://www.
    dw.com/en/lake-chad-climate-change-fosters-terrorism/
    a-18899499.

30. News Agency of Nigeria, "Nigeria Releases Census of Goats,
    Sheep, Pigs, Other Livestocks in Country," *Premium Times*, June
    2, 2016, http://www.premiumtimesng.com/news/top-news/
    204577-nigeria-releases-census-goats-sheep-pigs-livestocks-
    country.html; Roger Blench, "The Nigerian National Livestock
    Resource Survey: A Personal Account," http://horizon.
    documentation.ird.fr/exl-doc/pleins_textes/pleins_textes_7/
    divers2/010020164.pdf; National Bureau of Statistics, Nigeria,
    Harmonized Nigeria Living Standard Survey, 10: Core Welfare
    Indicator Questionnaire Survey 2009 (Part A), (2009), http://
    www.nigerianstat.gov.ng/pdfuploads/HARMONIZED%20
    NIGERIA%20LIVING%20STANDARD%20SURVEY%202009%20
    Part%20A.pdf.

31. Ken Henshaw and Fyneface D. Fyneface, *Seeing REDD:
    Communities, Forests, and Carbon Trading in Nigeria* (Port Harcourt:
    Social Development Integrated Centre [Social Action],
    2014), 3.

32. David-Chyddy Eleke, "The Menace of Erosion in Anambra," *This
    Day*, October 31, 2016, http://www.thisdaylive.com/index.php/
    2016/10/31/the-menace-of-erosion-in-anambra-2/.

33. R. J. Keenan et al., "Dynamics of Global Forest Area: Results from the FAO Global Forest Resources Assessment 2015," *Forest Ecology and Management* 352 (2015): 9–20, http://www.sciencedirect.com/science/article/pii/S0378112715003400.

34. Henshaw and Fyneface, *Seeing REDD*, 20.

35. Mark Amaza, "The Nigerian Super-Highway Project That Threatens a Million People's Homes," *Quartz Africa*, September 27, 2016, https://qz.com/791037/nigerias-cross-river-superhighway-received-buharis-blessing-but-has-run-into-environmental-concerns/.

36. *Nowhere to Run*, directed by Dan McCain (Core Productions, 2015), DVD.

37. Alex Abutu, "Report Exposes Misuse of Ecological Fund," *Daily Trust*, February 2, 2016, http://www.dailytrust.com.ng/news/environment/report-exposes-misuse-of-ecological-fund/131945.html.

38. International Centre for Investigative Reporting (Nigeria), "Ecological Funds: A Tale of Corruption and Waste," May 27, 2016, http://icirnigeria.org/main-headline-the-ecological-fund-of-corruption-and-misuse/.

39. Yinka Kolawole, "Nigeria Eyeing 1,000 MW of Electricity from Coal by 2020—Fayemi," *Vanguard*, March 20, 2016, http://www.vanguardngr.com/2016/03/nigeria-eyeing-1000-mw-electricity-coal-2020-fayemi/.

40. Roseline Okere, "Nigeria Burns off $5 Billion Resources Yearly from Gas Flaring," *The Guardian* (Nigeria), November 6, 2015, http://guardian.ng/features/weekend/nigeria-burns-off-5-billion-resources-yearly-from-gas-flaring/.

41. Tim Worstall, "Peak Oil Was Correct—It's Just It Was Peak Demand, Not Peak Supply," *Forbes*, November 28, 2016, https://www.forbes.com/sites/timworstall/201.

42. Occo Roelofsen, Namit Sharma, Rembrandt Sutorius, and Christer Tryggestad, "Is Peak Oil Demand in Sight?," McKinsey and Company *Oil and Gas* (blog), June 2016, http://www.mckinsey.com/industries/oil-and-gas/our-insights/is-peak-oil-demand-in-sight.

43. Michael Lynch, "Shale Oil Didn't Kill Off Peak Oil," *Forbes*, October 4, 2016, https://www.forbes.com/sites/michaellynch/2016/10/04/shale-oil-didnt-kill-off-peak-oil.

44. "Barrel Breakdown," *Wall Street Journal*, April 15, 2016, http://graphics.wsj.com/oil-barrel-breakdown/.
45. "Petrochemical Demand for Oil Set to Hold through to 2021—IEA," ICIS, February 22, 2016, https://www.icis.com/resources/news/2016/02/22/9972119/petrochemical-demand-for-oil-set-to-hold-through-to-2021-iea/#.
46. Annegret Mähler, "Nigeria: A Prime Example of the Resource Curse? Revisiting the Oil-Violence Link in the Niger Delta," German Institute of Global and Area Studies (GIGA), January 2010, 29, https://www.giga-hamburg.de/en/system/files/publications/wp120_maehler.pdf.
47. Kolade Larewaju, "Obasanjo Explodes—April Polls Do or Die Affair for PDP," *Vanguard*, February 11, 2007, http://allafrica.com/stories/200702110015.html.

FURTHER READING

Chapter 1: Historical Background

Achebe, Chinua. *There Was a Country: A Personal History of Biafra.* London: Penguin, 2013.

Alagoa, Ebiegheri Joe. *A History of the Niger Delta.* Port Harcourt: Onyoma Research Publications, 2005.

Amadi, Elechi. *Sunset in Biafra.* Oxford: Heinemann, 1973.

Bourne, Richard. *Nigeria: A New History of a Turbulent Century.* London: Zed Books, 2015.

Carland, John M. *The Colonial Office and Nigeria, 1898–1914.* Stanford, CA: Hoover Institution Press, 1985.

Cohen, Ronald. *The Kanuri of Bornu.* New York: Holt, Rinehart and Winston, 1967.

Cunliffe-Jones, Peter. *My Nigeria: Five Decades of Independence.* New York: St. Martin's Press, 2014.

De St. Jorre, John. *A Brother's War: Biafra and Nigeria.* London: Faber and Faber, 2009.

Diamond, Larry. *Class, Ethnicity, and Democracy in Nigeria: The Failure of the First Republic.* Syracuse, NY: Syracuse University Press, 1988.

Falola, Toyin, and Matthew Heaton. *A History of Nigeria.* New York: Cambridge University Press, 1999.

Hare, John. *Last Man In: The End of Empire in Northern Nigeria.* Tenterden, Kent, UK: Neville & Harding, 2013.

Joseph, Richard A. *Democracy and Prebendal Politics in Nigeria: The Rise and Fall of the Second Republic.* New York: Cambridge University Press, 2014.

Maier, Karl. *This House Has Fallen: Nigeria in Crisis.* London: Penguin, 2002.

Obasanjo, Olusegun. *My Command: An Account of the Nigerian Civil War 1967–1970*. Oxford: Heinemann, 1980.

Osaghae, Eghosa E. *Crippled Giant: Nigeria Since Independence*. Bloomington: Indiana University Press, 1998.

Paden, John. *Ahmadu Bello, Sardauna of Sokoto: Values and Leadership in Nigeria*. Zaria: Hudahuda Publishing, 1986.

Siollun, Max. *Nigeria's Military Coup Culture 1966–76: Oil Politics and Violence*. New York: Algora Publishing, 2009.

Siollun, Max. *Soldiers of Fortune: Nigerian Politics from Buhari to Babangida 1983–1993*. Abuja: Cassava Republic Press, 2013.

Smith, Robert S. *Kingdoms of the Yoruba*. 3rd ed. Madison: University of Wisconsin Press, 1988.

Chapter 2: The Economics of Oil

Gillies, Alexandra, Aaron Sayne, and Christina Katsouris. *Inside NNPC Oil Sales: A Case for Reform in Nigeria*. New York: Natural Resource Governance Institute, 2015. http://www.resourcegovernance.org/analysis-tools/publications/inside-nnpc-oil-sales-case-reform-nigeria.

Jerven, Morten. *Africa: Why Economists Get It Wrong*. London: Zed Books, 2015.

Katsouris, Christina, and Aaron Sayne. *Nigeria's Criminal Crude: International Options to Combat the Export of Stolen Oil*. London: Chatham House, 2013. https://www.chathamhouse.org/publications/papers/view/194254.

Lewis, Peter. *Growing Apart: Oil, Politics, and Economic Change in Indonesia and Nigeria*. Ann Arbor: University of Michigan Press, 2007.

Massachusetts Institute of Technology. *Observatory of Economic Complexity—Nigeria*. http://atlas.media.mit.edu/en/profile/country/nga/.

Nigerian National Bureau of Statistics e-Library. http://nigerianstat.gov.ng/library.

Nwokeji, Gilbert. *The Nigerian National Petroleum Corporation and the Development of the Nigerian Oil and Gas Industry: History, Strategy and Current Directions*. Houston, TX: James Baker Institute for Public Policy, Rice University, 2007. http://www.bakerinstitute.org/media/files/page/9b067dc6/noc_nnpc_ugo.pdf.

Ovadia, Jesse Salah. *The Petro-Developmental State in Africa: Making Oil Work in Angola, Nigeria, and the Gulf of Guinea*. London: C. Hurst and Co., 2016.

Page, Matthew. *Nigeria's Future Hinges on Its States*. New York: Council on Foreign Relations, 2016. http://www.cfr.org/nigeria/nigerias-future-hinges-its-states/p37437.

PwC. *Impact of Corruption on Nigeria's Economy*. Lagos: PwC, 2016. https://www.pwc.com/ng/en/assets/pdf/impact-of-corruption-on-nigerias-economy.pdf.

The State of the States: 2015. Lagos: BudgIT, 2016. http://yourbudgit.com/wp-content/uploads/2016/01/THE-FATE-OF-STATES-Final1.pdf.

Thurber, Mark C., Ifeyinwa M. Emelife, and Patrick R. P. Heller. *NNPC and Nigeria's Oil Patronage Ecosystem*. Stanford, CA: Stanford University, 2010. https://fsi.stanford.edu/sites/default/files/WP_95,_Thurber_Emelife_Heller,_NNPC,_16_September_2010.pdf.

United Nations Development Program. *National Human Development Report, 2015: Nigeria*. http://hdr.undp.org/sites/default/files/2016_national_human development_report_for_nigeria.pdf.

United States Energy Information Administration. *Country Analysis Brief: Nigeria*. May 6, 2016. https://www.eia.gov.

Usman, Zainab. *The Successes and Failures of Economic Reform in Nigeria's Post-Military Political Settlement*. Oxford: University of Oxford Global Economics and Governance Program, 2016. http://www.geg.ox.ac.uk/successes-and-failures-economic-reform-nigeria%E2%80%99s post-military-political-settlement.

Utomi, Patrick. "Nigeria as an Economic Powerhouse: Can It Be Achieved?" In *Crafting the New Nigeria*, edited by Robert Rotberg, 125–137. Boulder, CO: Lynne Reinner, 2004.

Chapter 3: Religion

Campbell, John. "Religion and Security in Nigeria." in *The Routledge Handbook of Religion and Security*, edited by Chris Seiple, Dennis R. Hoover, and Pauletta Otis, 215–225. London: Routledge, 2013.

Enwerem, Iheanyi. *Crossing the Rubicon: A Socio-Political Analysis of Political Catholicism in Nigeria*. Ibadan: Book-Builders, 2010.

Jenkins, Philip. *The Next Christendom: The Coming of Global Christianity*. 3rd ed. New York: Oxford University Press, 2011.

Kendhammer, Brandon. *Muslims Talking Politics: Framing Islam, Democracy, and Law in Northern Nigeria*. Chicago: University of Chicago Press, 2016.

Laremont, Ricardo Rene. *Islamic Law and Politics in Northern Nigeria*. Trenton, NJ: Africa World Press, 2011.

Marshall, Ruth. *Political Spiritualities: The Pentecostal Revolution in Nigeria*. Chicago: University of Chicago Press, 2009.

Paden, John. *Faith and Politics in Nigeria: Nigeria as a Pivotal State in the Muslim World*. Washington, DC: United States Institute of Peace, 2008.

Paden, John. *Muslim Civic Cultures and Conflict Resolution: The Challenges of Democratic Federalism in Nigeria*. Washington, DC: Brookings Institution Press, 2006.

Thurston, Alexander. *Salafism in Nigeria: Islam, Preaching, and Politics*. Cambridge, UK: Cambridge University Press, 2016.

Vaughan, Olufemi. *Religion and the Making of Nigeria*. Durham, NC: Duke University Press, 2016.

Wariboko, Nimi. *Nigerian Pentecostalism*. Rochester, NY: University of Rochester Press, 2014.

Chapter 4: Politics: Nigeria's Great Game

Adebanwi, Wale. *Nation as Grand Narrative: The Nigerian Press and the Politics of Meaning*. Rochester, NY: University of Rochester Press, 2016.

Adeniyi, Olusegun. *Against the Run of Play: How an Incumbent President Was Defeated in Nigeria*. Lagos: Prestige/This Day Press, 2017.

Adeniyi, Olusegun. *Power, Politics, and Death: A Front Row Account of Nigeria under the Late President Yar'Adua*. Lagos: Prestige, 2011.

Agbiboa, Daniel Egiegba. "Serving the Few, Starving the Many: How Corruption Underdevelops Nigeria and How There Is an Alternative Perspective to Corruption Cleanups." *Africa Today* 58 (2012): 111–132.

Ajayi, Rotimi, and Joseph Olayinka Fashagba, eds. *Understanding Government and Politics in Nigeria*. Omu-Aran, Nigeria: Landmark University, 2014.

Chayes, Sarah. *Thieves of State: Why Corruption Threatens Global Security*. New York: W. W. Norton and Company, 2015. See chapter 10.

Enahoro, Peter. *How to Be a Nigerian*. Ibadan: Mosuro, 2013.

Human Rights Watch. *Corruption on Trial? The Record of Nigeria's Economic and Financial Crimes Commission*. New York: Human Rights Watch, 2011. https://www.hrw.org/sites/default/files/reports/nigeria0811WebToPost.pdf.

"International Thief-Thief": How British Banks Are Complicit in Nigerian Corruption. London: Global Witness, 2010. https://www.globalwitness.org/documents/14080/international_thief_thief_final.pdf.

Kendhammer, Brandon. "Talking Ethnic but Hearing Multi-ethnic: The Peoples' Democratic Party (PDP) in Nigeria and Durable Multi-ethnic Parties in the Midst of Violence." *Commonwealth & Comparative Politics* 48, no. 1 (February 2010): 48–71.

Kew, Darren. "Nigerian Elections and the Neopatrimonial Paradox: In Search of the Social Contract." *Journal of Contemporary African Studies* 28, no. 4 (October 2010): 499–521.

LeVan, A. Carl. *Dictators and Democracy in African Development: The Political Economy of Good Governance in Nigeria*. New York: Cambridge University Press, 2015.

Liebowitz, Jeremy, and Jibrin Ibrahim. *A Capacity Assessment of Nigerian Political Parties*. Abuja: United Nations Development Program, 2013.

Owen, Olly, and Zainab Usman. "Briefing: Why Goodluck Jonathan Lost of the Nigerian Presidential Election of 2015." *African Affairs* 114 (2015): 455–471.

Page, Matthew T. *Improving U.S. Anticorruption Policy in Nigeria*. New York: Council on Foreign Relations, 2016.

Rotberg, Robert, ed. *Crafting the New Nigeria*. Boulder, CO: Lynne Reinner, 2004.

Smith, Daniel Jordan. *A Culture of Corruption: Everyday Deception and Popular Discontent in Nigeria*. Princeton, NJ: Princeton University Press, 2010.

Suberu, Rotimi T. *Federalism and Ethnic Conflict in Nigeria*. Washington, DC: United States Institute of Peace, 2001.

Williams, Pat Ama Tokunbo. "Women and the Dilemma of Politics in Nigeria." In *Dilemmas of Democracy in Nigeria*, edited by Paul A. Beckett and Crawford Young, 219–241. Rochester, NY: University of Rochester Press, 1997.

Chapter 5: Nigeria's Security Challenges

Abubakar, Fati (@bitsofborno) via Twitter and Instagram.

Adunbi, Omolade. *Oil Wealth and Insurgency in Nigeria*. Bloomington: University of Indiana Press, 2015.

Agbiboa, Daniel Egiegba. "Protectors or Predators? The Embedded Problem of Police Corruption and Deviance in Nigeria." *Administration and Society* 47 (2015): 244–281.

Amnesty International. *Killing at Will: Extrajudicial Executions and Other Unlawful Killings by the Police in Nigeria*. London: Amnesty International, 2009. https://www.amnesty.org/en/documents/AFR44/038/2009/en/.

Asuni, Judith Burdin. *Understanding the Armed Groups of the Niger Delta*. New York: Council on Foreign Relations, 2009. http://i.cfr. org/content/publications/attachments/CFR_WorkingPaper_2_ NigerDelta.pdf.

Bagu, Chom, and Katie Smith. *Past Is Prologue: Criminality and Reprisal Violence in Nigeria's Middle Belt*. Washington, DC: Search for Common Ground, 2017. https://www.sfcg.org/wp-content/ uploads/2017/04/Criminality-Reprisal-Attack-dr-2.pdf.

Barkindo, Atta. *How Boko Haram Exploits History and Memory*. London: Africa Research Institute, 2016. http://www. africaresearchinstitute.org/newsite/publications/boko-haram-exploits-history-memory/.

Bassey, Celestine O., and Charles Q. Dokubo. *Defence Policy of Nigeria: Capability and Context*. Bloomington, IN: AuthorHouse, 2011.

@beegeagleblog on Twitter.

Comolli, Virginia. *Boko Haram: Nigeria's Islamist Insurgency*. London: C. Hurst and Company, 2015.

Courson, Elias. *Movement for the Emancipation of the Niger Delta (MEND): Political Marginalization, Repression and Petro-insurgency in the Niger Delta*. Uppsala: Nordiska Afrikainstitutet, 2009. http:// www.diva-portal.org/smash/get/diva2%3A280470/FULLTEXT01. pdf.

Curbing Violence in Nigeria (I): The Jos Crisis. Washington, DC: International Crisis Group, 2012. https://www.crisisgroup.org/ africa/west-africa/nigeria/curbing-violence-nigeria-i-jos-crisis.

Doron, Ray, and Toyin Falola. *Ohio Short Histories of Africa: Ken Saro-Wiwa*. Athens: Ohio University Press, 2016.

Ellis, Stephen. *This Present Darkness: A History of Nigerian Organized Crime*. Oxford: Oxford University Press, 2016.

Guttschuss, Eric. *"Leave Everything to God": Accountability for Inter-Communal Violence in Plateau and Kaduna States, Nigeria*. Washington, DC: Human Rights Watch, 2013. https://www.hrw.org/sites/ default/files/reports/nigeria1213_ForUpload.pdf.

Higazi, Adam. "Social Mobilization and Collective Violence: Vigilantes and Militias in the Lowlands of Plateau State, Central Nigeria." *Africa: Journal of the International African Institute* 78 (2008): 107–135.

Human Rights Watch. *Politics as War: The Human Rights Impact and Causes of Post-Election Violence in Rivers State, Nigeria*. Washington, DC: Human Rights Watch, 2008. https://www.hrw.org/reports/ 2008/nigeria0308/.

Kassim, Abdulbasit, and Michael Nwankpa, eds. *The Boko Haram Reader: From Nigerian Preachers to the Islamic State.* London: Hurst, 2017.

Matfess, Hilary. *Women and the War on Boko Haram: Wives, Weapons, Witnesses.* London: Zed Books, 2017.

Middle Belt, Not Killing Belt: The History, Dynamics, and Political Dimensions of Ethno-Religious Conflicts in the Middle Belt. Abuja: ActionAid, 2008. www.actionaid.org/sites/files/actionaid/middle_belt1.pdf.

Nigeria: The Challenge of Military Reform. Washington, DC: International Crisis Group, 2016. https://www.crisisgroup.org/africa/west-africa/nigeria/nigeria-challenge-military-reform.

Nwajiaku-Dahou, Kathryn. *The Niger Delta Amnesty: Lessons Four Years On.* Abuja: Nigeria Stability and Reconstruction Programme, 2014. http://www.nsrp-nigeria.org/wp-content/uploads/2014/11/E189-NSRP-Policy-Brief-ND-Amnesty-4-Yrs-On_FINAL_web.pdf.

Ogbozor, Ernest. *Understanding the Informal Security Sector in Nigeria.* Washington, DC: United States Institute of Peace, 2016. http://www.usip.org/publications/2016/09/15/understanding-the-informal-security-sector-in-nigeria.

Okonta, Ike, and Oronto Douglas. *Where Vultures Feast: Shell, Human Rights, and Oil in the Niger Delta.* New York: Verso, 2003.

Ostien, Philip. *Jang and the Jasawa: Ethno-Religious Conflict in Jos, Nigeria.* Bayreuth: University of Bayreuth, 2009. http://www.sharia-in-africa.net/pages/publications/jonah-jang-and-the-jasawa-ethno-religious-conflict-in-jos-nigeria.php.

Owen, Olly. *The Nigeria Police Force: Predicaments and Possibilities.* Oxford: University of Oxford Nigeria Research Network, 2014. http://www3.qeh.ox.ac.uk/pdf/nrn/nrn-wp15.pdf.

Peel, Michael. *A Swamp Full of Dollars: Pipelines and Paramilitaries at Nigeria's Oil Frontier.* London: I. B. Tauris, 2009.

Pérouse de Montclos, Marc-Antoine. *Nigeria's Interminable Insurgency? Addressing the Boko Haram Crisis.* London: Chatham House, 2014. https://www.chathamhouse.org/sites/files/chathamhouse/field/field_document/20140901BokoHaramPerousedeMontclos_0.pdf.

Policing Communal Conflicts: The State, Parallel Security Providers, and Communities. Oxford: Nigeria Research Network, 2013. http://www3.qeh.ox.ac.uk/pdf/nrn/nrn-pb04.pdf.

Pratten, David. "The Politics of Protection: Perspectives on Vigilantism in Nigeria." *Africa: Journal of the International African Institute* 78 (2008): 1–15.

Stakeholder Democracy Network. "Review of Niger Delta Community Perceptions on Conflict, Militancy and Change: Does Violence Pay?" 2013. http://www.stakeholderdemocracy.org/does-violence-pay-community-perceptions-of-violence/.

Stars on Their Shoulders, Blood on Their Hands: War Crimes Committed by the Nigerian Military. London: Amnesty International, 2015. https://www.amnesty.org/en/documents/afr44/1657/2015/en/.

The Imam and the Pastor. Directed by Alan Channer. FLT Films, 2009. DVD.

Thurston, Alex. *'The Disease Is Unbelief': Boko Haram's Religious and Political Worldview.* Washington, DC: Brookings Institution, 2016. https://www.brookings.edu/wp-content/uploads/2016/07/Brookings-Analysis-Paper_Alex-Thurston_Final_Web.pdf.

Transparency International. *Government Defence Anti-Corruption Index 2015: Nigeria.* London: Transparency International, 2015. https://government.defenceindex.org/countries/nigeria/.

Walker, Andrew. *"Eat the Heart of the Infidel": The Harrowing of Nigeria and the Rise of Boko Haram.* London: C. Hurst and Company, 2016.

Watching Us Die on CNN: Report on the Study of Community-level Conflict Management Mechanisms in the Niger Delta, Middle Belt and North East Zones of Nigeria. Abuja: Nigeria Stability and Reconciliation Programme, 2012. www.nsrp-nigeria.org/wp-content/uploads/2014/08/E190-CCMM-Studies-Web.pdf.

Watts, Michael. "Blood Oil: The Anatomy of a Petro-Insurgency in the Niger Delta." *Focaal—European Journal of Anthropology* 52 (2008): 18–38.

Chapter 6: Nigeria and the World

Abegunrin, Olayiwola. *Nigerian Foreign Policy Under Military Rule 1966–1999.* Westport, CT: Praeger, 2003.

Achebe, Chinua. *Things Fall Apart.* London: Penguin, 2006.

Adebajo, Adekeye, and Abdul Raufu Mustapha, eds. *Gulliver's Troubles: Nigeria's Foreign Policy after the Cold War.* Scottsville, South Africa: University of KwaZulu-Natal Press, 2008.

Blanchard, Lauren Ploch, and Tomas F. Husted. *Nigeria: Current Issues and U.S. Policy.* Washington, DC: Congressional Research Service, 2016.

Campbell, John. *Nigeria: Dancing on the Brink.* upd. ed. Lanham, MD: Rowman and Littlefield, 2013.

Cole, Teju. *Open City.* New York: Faber and Faber, 2011.

Garba, Joe. *Diplomatic Soldiering: The Conduct of Nigerian Foreign Policy 1975–1979*. Ibadan: Spectrum Books, 1987.

Soyinka, Wole. *King Baabu*. London: Methuen, 2002.

Chapter 7: Nigeria of the Future

Alexa.com. Internet traffic analysis for Nigeria. http://www.alexa.com/topsites/countries/NG/.

Bloch, R., S. Fox, J. Monroy, and A. Ojo. *Urbanisation and Urban Expansion in Nigeria: Urbanisation Research Nigeria (URN) Research Report*. London: ICF International, 2015. http://urn.icfwebservices.com/Media/Default/Publications/URN%20Theme%20A%20Urbanisation%20Report%20FINAL.pdf.

@BudgITng on Twitter.

de Gramont, Diane. *Governing Lagos: Unlocking the Politics of Reform*. Washington, DC: Carnegie Endowment for International Peace, 2015.

@DrJoeAbah (Dr. Joe Abah, Director-General, Bureau of Public Service Reforms) on Twitter.

Eddings, Jerri. "The Power of Social Media in the Nigerian Election." International Center for Journalists, April 20, 2015. https://www.icfj.org/blogs/power-social-media-nigerian-election.

Fourchard, Laurent. *Understanding Slums: Case Studies for the Global Report 2003 - Ibadan, Nigeria*. London: University College London, 2003. http://www.ucl.ac.uk/dpu-projects/Global_Report/pdfs/Ibadan.pdf.

@FutureLagos on Twitter.

LeVan, A. Carl, and Josiah Olubowale. "'I Am Here until Development Comes': Displacement, Demolitions, and Property Rights in Urbanizing Nigeria." *African Affairs* 113 (2014): 387–408.

National Population Commission (Nigeria). *Nigeria Demographic and Health Survey 2013*. Abuja: National Population Commission, 2014. https://dhsprogram.com/pubs/pdf/FR293/FR293.pdf.

Nigerian Bureau of Statistics. *Nigeria Poverty Profile 2010*. Abuja: Nigerian Bureau of Statistics, 2012. http://www.nigerianstat.gov.ng/pdfuploads/Nigeria%20Poverty%20Profile%202010.pdf.

Nowhere to Run. Directed by Dan McCain. Core Productions, 2015. DVD.

"The Oil Conundrum." *The Economist*, January 23, 2016. http://www.economist.com/news/briefing/21688919-plunging-prices-have-neither-halted-oil-production-nor-stimulated-surge-global-growth.

Oloyede, Olaoluwa. "Nigerian Mobile Trends 2017." *Jumia* (blog), April 19, 2017, https://blog.jumia.com.ng/jumia-unveils-third-white-paper-nigerian-mobile-trends-2017/.

Premium Times. http://www.premiumtimesng.com/. @ PremiumTimesNG on Twitter.

Roelofsen, Occo, Namit Sharma, Rembrandt Sutorius, and Christer Tryggestad. "Is Peak Oil Demand in Sight?" McKinsey and Company *Oil and Gas* (blog), June 2016. http://www.mckinsey.com/industries/oil-and-gas/our-insights/is-peak-oil-demand-in-sight.

The Social Media Landscape in Nigeria. Lagos: Africa Practice, 2014. http://www.africapractice.com/wp-content/uploads/2014/04/Africa-Practice-Social-Media-Landscape-Vol-1.pdf.

"Special Report: Nigeria—After Oil." *The Economist*, June 18, 2015. http://www.economist.com/news/special-report/21654361-oil-shock-has-left-deep-hole-governments-finances-economy.

United Nations Department of Economic and Social Affairs/Population Division. *World Population Prospects: The 2015 Revision, Key Findings and Advance Tables*. New York: United Nations, 2015. https://esa.un.org/unpd/wpp/publications/files/key_findings_wpp_2015.pdf.

United Nations Environmental Program. *Environmental Assessment of Ogoniland*. http://postconflict.unep.ch/publications/OEA/UNEP_OEA.pdf.

United Nations Framework Convention on Climate Change. "Nigeria's Intended Nationally Determined Contribution." November 27, 2015. http://www4.unfccc.int/submissions/INDC/Published%20Documents/Nigeria/1/Approved%20Nigeria's%20INDC_271115.pdf.

Whiteman, Kaye. *Lagos: City of the Imagination*. Abuja: Cassava Republic, 2014.

INDEX

Page numbers followed by n indicate notes.

31901064643168